Basic Parliamentary Procedure Workbook

Fifth Edition

A Basic Course in Parliamentary Procedure

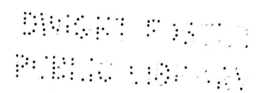
Joyce L. Stephens

Frederick Publishers
Clearwater, Florida

BASIC PARLIAMENTARY PROCEDURE WORKBOOK
A BASIC COURSE IN PARLIAMENTARY PROCEDURE
FIFTH EDITION

Copyright © 1984, 1986, 1990, 1992, 1994 by
Joyce L. Stephens
ISBN 0-9629765-4-7
Glossary
Bibliography
Reading List

Frederick Publishers
P. O. Box 5043
Clearwater, FL 34618
813-530-3978

Printing brokered by Robert M. Hough, Tampa, Florida
Printed in the United States of America

Basic Parliamentary Procedure
Workbook

Drawings by Heidi Tilney
Heidi's drawings of Woodrow the eager beaver have been so popular we have repeated them in this edition of the Workbook.
Fourth Edition edited by Marjorie Humphreys Park

In this fifth edition the changes in the format of the quizzes will make the book easier to use. The author is grateful to all who have made suggestions for this fifth edition of the workbook. Your suggestions have helped to make each edition better than the last. Anyone is welcome to comment on the books at any time. Write to the author in care of the publisher.

The author's other books which are internationally distributed, *Guide for the Presiding Officer* and *Guide to Voting Procedures* will be joined by *Guide to Great Meetings* in 1994.

Notes from the author

This fifth edition of the Workbook is expanded from previous editions in examples and quizzes. Much of the correspondence that the author and publisher have received about the book has been about these two sections. New quizzes are included for those teachers of parliamentary procedure who have used the book for many years in their classes through several editions.

The book is used throughout the United States in high schools, colleges, clubs, associations, and local governmental bodies for basic instruction in parliamentary rules. You might have become familiar with it during a visit to your local library. Internationally, the book is now known in Canada, Mexico, Germany and other European countries. We have been very gratified at the response in this regard.

The author is very pleased to present this fifth edition. There is an evident need for basic instruction in this important subject. Young people begin to learn about government very early in school, and soon learn that democracy can be achieved easily in their clubs by the use of parliamentary procedure.

During the process of learning parliamentary procedure students of all ages gain self-confidence in public speaking and making logical and persuasive statements in debate. The study of parliamentary procedure is valuable in the development of future community leaders.

Basic Parliamentary Procedure Workbook

A Basic Course in Parliamentary Procedure

How To Use This Book

1) Read the prepared text, Section One.

2) Find Key words and phrases in the text or in the glossary.

3) Refer to Examples, Section Two, for the portion of the text you are studying.

3) Test your knowledge, using the Quizzes in Section Three.

4) Check your answers to the quizzes by rereading the text, or use the Answer Key on page 111.

- Two charts are provided for ready reference to the rules relating to motions.

- The Glossary will help you to learn parliamentary terminology.

- Language of the Presiding Officer, page 73, gives the correct wording for chairing a meeting and handling motions.

- Where key words or phrases are given, look them up in the text or the glossary for a better understanding.

- This workbook is a basic course. For more information and a more advanced explanation of all the parliamentary rules, consult *Robert's Rules of Order Newly Revised.*

This workbook is designed for beginners in parliamentary procedure and others who have had classes in the past and who want to sharpen their meeting skills. The text is basic, or elementary, parliamentary procedure. For new presidents, *Guide For the Presiding Officer* is available. See order form at the back of this book.

A Professional Registered Parliamentarian is an expert in parliamentary rules and procedure who can help the student to understand parliamentary procedure as used by modern organizations.

Contents

Contents

Table of Motions

Section One

Text

For unfamiliar words and phrases used in the text,
see Glossary, page 117.

RONR = *Robert's Rules of Order Newly Revised,*
1990 Edition

PARLIAMENTARY LAW

Parliamentary Law is the body of enacted rules and
recognized usages which govern the procedure
of deliberative assemblies.

PARLIAMENTARY PROCEDURE

Parliamentary procedure is a logical procedure for
the implementation
of parliamentary law in meetings.

• PRINCIPLES •

- Rule of the majority
- Right of the minority to be heard
- Equality of opinion
- Protection of absentees
- One subject at a time

• PURPOSES •

- Orderly conduct of business
- Protection of the rights of members
- Decorum in debate
- Solid foundation for resolving
  questions of procedure

DECORUM

Decorum is simply good manners. Good behavior is essential to productive meetings, large or small. When members are courteous but formal, even in situations of great disagreement, there will be no disruptions of meetings because of ill temper.

The Chair is addressed as *Mr.* or *Madam Chairman* or *Mr.* or *Madam President.* One does not address the Chair by his or her name. The presiding officer refers to himself as *The Chair,* never *I.* When the president is reporting on his activities in behalf of the organization he may say "Your *President reports...."*

A vice-president while presiding is addressed as *Mr. President* unless the president is in the room. Then he is addressed as *Mr. Chairman.*

Members do not speak in assemblies until they have obtained the floor (been recognized by the Chair), except for a few motions which do not require recognition.

Members address their remarks through the chair, not directly to each other, and never question the motives of another member.

In debate, the discussion is on the pending question. All remarks must be germane to the immediately pending question.

The Chair usually addresses the member as *the member* unless the member is presenting a report or has risen to be recognized.

Members should not complain after a meeting that "something was done incorrectly." It is a member's duty to raise a point of order at the time of the breach of order instead of complaining about it later.

Members must not disturb other members by talking among themselves or walking around the room after the meeting has begun.

Members who arrive late to meetings should sit in the first available seat without disturbing the assembly. Members who arrive late should never walk into the assembly while a prayer is being offered, or while a vote is being counted.

Those who are to be seated at the head table should arrive a few minutes early so that there are no vacant chairs when the meeting begins, and no one attracts the attention of the assembly by arriving late.

A committee on protocol may be appointed to help the president with the seating of officers and program presenters in the most appropriate places, and to extend proper courtesies to guests.

It is the duty of members to be in their seats at the time the meeting is to begin, and it is the duty of the Chair to call the meeting to order on time.

Key words and phrases:
decorum
protocol
chair
recognized
through the chair
germane
point of order
duty

ORDER OF BUSINESS

1. Call to order
2. Opening exercises (Optional)
3. Reading and approval of the minutes
4. Reports of officers, boards, and standing committees
5. Reports of special committees
6. Special Orders
7. Unfinished business and General Orders
8. New business
9. Announcements
10. Adjournment

How the Chair Handles the Order of Business

1. **Call to order.** With one rap of the gavel the chair calls the meeting to order: "The meeting will come to order." It is the duty of the chair to call the meeting to order on time.

2. **Opening exercises.** The invocation or prayer always precedes the Pledge of Allegiance to the Flag, after which any other opening exercises are in order.

3. **Reading and approval of the minutes.** 'Robert's Rules' begins the order of business here. "The secretary will read the minutes of the previous meeting." "Are there any corrections to the minutes?" (avoid redundancies such as 'are there any corrections or additions') "Are there any further corrections to the minutes?" If no corrections: "The minutes are approved as read."
If corrections: "The minutes are approved as corrected."

4. **Reports of officers, boards, and standing committees.** The officers and standing committees report in the order in which they are listed in the bylaws. The Report of the Treasurer goes here. "The next business in order is the Treasurer's report. (or Financial Report.)" "Are there any questions on the Treasurer's report?" "The report will be filed." "The next business in order is reports of standing committees. Mrs. Andrews will report for the ... committee."

5. **Reports of special committees.** Only those scheduled to report should be called upon. "The special committee on ... will report.—Mr. Johnson."

6. **Special orders.***

   "At the (date) meeting the motion "..." was made a special order for this meeting. The chair recognizes Mr. Fortune."

   * Matters which the bylaws require to be considered at a particular meeting are also Special Orders.[1]

7. **Unfinished business and General orders.***

   The chair does not ask for unfinished business. The chair will know whether something was postponed until this meeting. "At the September meeting consideration of ... was postponed to this meeting." Is there any discussion?"

   * Bylaw amendments are also General orders.[2]

   See: General Orders and Special Orders, pp. 49, 50.

8. **New business.** "Is there any new business?" (See text for handling motions.)

9. **Announcements.** "Are there any announcements?"

10. **Adjournment.** "If there is no objection and no further business the meeting will be adjourned." "Since there is no objection and no further business, the meeting is adjourned." *or* "The Chair declares the meeting adjourned."

    Test Yourself page 83, #1 and #2

Items may be added to the agenda in the appropriate places. The order of business is a generic agenda. This is usually used when the meeting is small with little business to consider. If the meeting is large or complicated, the agenda will have additional items, sometimes in great detail. All items of business will come up under a class of business on the generic agenda.

An inexperienced presiding officer will find that a script agenda is helpful. For each item of business, the words used to introduce it and dispose of it are written in at particular places on the agenda.

---

[1] See *Robert's Rules of Order Newly Revised*, 1990 Edition (RONR), pp. 182, 351

[2] See RONR, p. 589

Agenda for Annual Meeting or Convention

An order of business or agenda for an annual meeting or convention is often called a program and includes events.

Basic example of a *convention* program:

Key words and phrases:
agenda
order of business
program
convention
annual meeting
sine die

Program
Bonny Society Annual Convention
June 8-9, 1999
June 8

9:00 A.M.   Call to order
            Opening exercises
            Report of the Credentials Committee (Maj. vote)
            Report of the Standing Rules Committee (2/3 vote)
            Report of the Program Committee (Maj. vote)
            Appointment of Meeting Committees
            Reports of Officers
            Report of the Board of Directors
            Reports of Standing Committees
            Reports of Special Committees
            Report of the Nominating Committee
            Election of Officers, Directors
            Adjourn

December 8

12:30 P.M. Luncheon
            Speaker
 1:30 P.M. Educational workshops
 6:00 P.M. Reception
 8:00 P.M. Banquet

December 9

 9:00 A.M. Educational workshops
12:00 M.   Luncheon
 1:00 P.M. Reconvene
            Report of the Elections Committee
            Amendment of bylaws
            Report of the Resolutions Committee
            New Business
            Announcements
            Adjournment sine die

How to Complete Action on a Motion

1) The member rises, addresses the Chair: "Mr. (or) Madam President," and waits for recognition.

2) The Chair recognizes the member (grants him the floor).

3) The member makes a motion: "I move that...."

4) Another member seconds the motion.[1]

5) The Chair *states* the motion[2] and opens the floor to debate (on debatable motions). "It is moved and seconded that ...." "Is there any discussion?" *or* "Are you ready for the question?"

6) Members discuss the motion, after being granted the floor by the Chair.

7) After debate, the Chair repeats the motion and *puts* the question[3] (takes the vote). "The question is on the motion that .... Those in favor say *aye*. Those opposed, say *no*. The *ayes* have it and the motion is adopted."

Action on a motion is not complete until the Chair has announced the result of the vote.

Note: When a committee reports, the reporting member moves the adoption of a motion to implement any recommendations contained in the report. Committee motions and resolutions do not require a second.

Test Yourself, page 84, #3

Key words and phrases:
address the chair
recognize
second
state the motion
debate
put the question
action

---

[1] See RONR, p. 34, footnote
[2] See RONR, pp. 31, 39
[3] See RONR, p. 43

Voting

- *Putting the question* means taking the vote.
- The usual method of voting is by voice (vive voce). The Chair should always take the *aye* vote and the *no* vote, and *announce* the result of the vote. EXCEPTION: The *no* vote is not usually taken on a courtesy resolution unless a member requests that the negative vote be taken. Sometimes the vote is taken by a show of hands.
- The motion *Call for a Division* or *Call for a Division of the Assembly* is a call for a *rising* vote. It can be demanded by a single member, without a second. The purpose of the motion is to verify a voice vote. On important or controversial questions the Chair, on his own initiative, may take a *counted rising vote,* or a member may make the motion to *have the vote counted.* The motion to *count the vote* requires a second and a majority vote to adopt. *NOTE:* A rising vote is taken on a motion requiring a two-thirds vote for adoption, unless it is a ballot vote.
- The Chair, if a member, may vote when his vote will affect the result—to break a tie, to create a tie, to prevent a two-thirds, to create a two-thirds. The Chair always votes when the vote is by ballot, but may not vote again to alter the result.
- A ballot vote is usually a written ballot, and it usually is a secret ballot. A vote to make a ballot vote *unanimous* must be taken by ballot, not by voice.

  A ballot vote may be taken on a motion as well as on an election. In that case the voter writes *yes* or *no* on the ballot. The ballot may be a blank piece of paper, or if the question is known in advance, the ballot may be printed with the proposal and with a place provided for affirmative and negative votes.

  See examples of tellers' reports for elections and other questions on pages 69–70.
- A member may vote against his motion, but he may not speak against it.

- Majority vote: More than half the votes cast[1]
  Plurality vote: The largest number of votes cast[2]
  Two-thirds vote: At least 2/3 of the votes cast[3]
  Unanimous vote: No dissenting votes[4]
  Tie vote: The same number of affirmative and negative votes[5]

Key words and phrases:
put the question
vive voce
courtesy resolution
division of the assembly
counted rising vote
ballot vote
announce
incidental

Test Yourself, page 91, #10.

---

[1] RONR, p. 395
[2] RONR, p. 399
[3] RONR, p. 396
[4] RONR, p. 406
[5] RONR, p. 400

Quorum

The *Quorum* is the minimum number of members who must be present at a meeting to constitute a legal meeting where business may be transacted. *If the bylaws do not specify otherwise,* a quorum is a majority of the members.[1]

When there is no quorum, the only business that may be transacted is:
- Fix the Time to Which to Adjourn
- Adjourn
- Recess
- Take measures to obtain a quorum.

Quorum should not be confused with the term *majority* as used in voting. A majority *vote* is a majority of those *present and voting, not* a majority of those present, and *not* a majority of the quorum.

For example: If a quorum is 25, and there are 30 present, it is possible that only 16 members will choose to vote on a motion. In that case, the majority *vote* is more than half the votes cast, or 9 (a majority of 16, those voting).

Key words and phrases:
quorum
majority
majority vote
legal meeting
legally adopted motion

Second

A second merely suggests that the seconder believes that the subject should be discussed.[2] It does not suggest that the seconder agrees with the motion. If a motion has been stated by the chair and debate has begun, the lack of a second is ignored. By debating the question, others have agreed that the motion should be discussed. If a motion which requires a second is adopted but has not been seconded, it *is* a legally adopted motion.

The maker of the motion is recorded in the minutes, but not the seconder unless the bylaws provide for it.

---

[1] RONR, pp.19-20
[2] RONR, pp. 35

Classes of Motions

• **Main Motion** - brings business before the assembly:

a. *An Original Main Motion* - introduces a *new* subject for consideration.

b. *An Incidental Main Motion* - is incidental to the business of the assembly.

An Incidental Main Motion does not bring a new subject for consideration. Some incidental main motions resemble motions of other classes, but differ in their rules and in when they may be introduced. See page 45.

• **Subsidiary Motions** - assist the assembly in disposing of the main motion. The subsidiary motions are: *to postpone indefinitely, to amend, to refer to a committee, to postpone to a definite time, to limit or extend limits of debate, to order the previous question, and to lay the question on the table.*

• **Privileged Motions** - are privileged because they relate to matters of special or immediate importance. The privileged motions are: *to call for the orders of the day, to raise a question of privilege, to recess, to adjourn, and to fix the time to which to adjourn.*

• **Incidental Motions** - relate to the pending business in some way. Incidental motions are shown on the chart on page 48.

• **Motions That Bring A Question Again Before The Assembly**: *Take From the Table, Amend Something Previously Adopted, Rescind, Discharge a Committee, Reconsider.*

Key words and phrases:
main motion
original main motion
incidental main motion
incidental motions
privileged motions
subsidiary motions

Precedence, or Rank of Motions

The *Main Motion,* the *Subsidiary Motions,* and the *Privileged Motions* fall into what is called *order of precedence,* and each has a rank to each other. The Main Motion is the lowest ranking of these 13 motions and the highest ranking is To Fix the Time to Which to Adjourn.

Key words and phrases:
precedence - rank
yield
ranking motions

Order of precedence tells the maker of a motion whether a certain motion is in order at that time.

Each motion has a proper place in the order, taking precedence of motions that rank below it. Motions yield to motions that rank above them.[1]

The 13 ranking motions are listed on the next page in the correct order of precedence or rank. For example: If an amendment to a main motion is pending, the motion to Postpone Indefinitely is not in order, but any motion above To Amend is in order. (See Chart on page 47.)

Incidental Motions have no rank among themselves and have no position of rank. When they are in order, they are handled immediately and rank above any other motions that are pending. Most are not debatable. (See Chart on page 48.)

Motions that Bring a Question Again Before the Assembly can usually be considered when no other business is pending. These motions are: *Reconsider, Take From the Table, Amend Something Previously Adopted, Rescind, and Discharge a Committee.*

---

[1] RONR, pp. 58-68

The
Thirteen Ranking Motions
in order of precedence, or rank,
beginning with the highest ranking are:

• Privileged Motions •
Fix the Time to Which to Adjourn **Adjourn** **Recess** **Raise a Question of Privilege** **Call for the Orders of the Day**
• Subsidiary Motions •
Lay the Question on the Table **Previous Question** **Limit or Extend Limits of Debate** **Postpone to a Certain Time** **Commit or Refer to a Committee** **Amend the Main Motion** **Postpone Indefinitely**
• Main Motion • **Main Motion**

Students studying for exams should memorize the
above list in order.

A chart of rules relating to these motions is on page 47.

The Main Motion

A *Main Motion* is a proposition that something be done, or that something is the opinion of the assembly.

An *Original Main Motion* brings before the assembly some new subject for consideration and action.

An *Incidental Main Motion* is a main motion that is incidental to the business of the assembly or to its previously taken action. (for example, to amend something previously adopted. See page 20.)

Key words and phrases:
resolution
conflict
invalid
session
primary amendment
secondary amendment
germane

Rules Concerning the Main Motion:

- It may be made when no other business is pending.
- It may not conflict with the bylaws, Articles of Incorporation, local, state or national law, or rules of a superior body. If it so conflicts and is adopted, it is invalid (null and void).
- It may not conflict with or be substantially the same as a motion previously adopted or rejected by the assembly during the same session, or a motion that has been introduced and has not been finally disposed of, or will come up under unfinished business.
- It may have applied to it any subsidiary motion, that is, it may be amended, committed, postponed, etc. It is the lowest ranking motion.
- A main motion, when possible, should be in the affirmative rather than the negative form.
- A main motion requires recognition by the chair. It requires a second, is debatable, requires a majority vote for adoption, and it may be reconsidered.
- A main motion is amendable. See *To Amend* page 27.
  A main motion may be amended to the first and second degrees. The primary amendment must be germane to the main motion, and the secondary amendment must be germane to the primary amendment. An amendment of the third degree is not in order. See *Is It Germane?* page 37.
- A main motion should be concise, unambiguous, and contain all of the information needed to carry through on the action proposed (what, when, where, how, who). Say what you mean in as few words as possible. Motions are entered into the minutes the way the chair states the motions.

•• To *Amend the Bylaws* is an Incidental Main motion which may be amended to the first and second degrees. There are special rules for amending the bylaws. This is a form of the Incidental Main Motion *To Amend Something Previously Adopted.* See pages 41 and 45.

Examples - Main Motion

"I move that the association hold an antique show and sale at Morris Convention Center, March 5–March 7 from 8:00 A.M. to 10:00 P.M. to raise money for our Children's Services Program."

"I move that the club hold a dance to raise funds for the book fund, and that a Fund Raising Committee be in charge of arrangements."

"I move that the club purchase a computer for the secretary, at a cost not to exceed $3000."

"I move that the Bird Watcher's League provide binoculars for each Junior member, and that the cost be included in next year's budget."

"I move that the chapter appoint a membership committee with the charge to increase our student membership."

"I move that all our official publications carry our club motto on the front cover."

"I move that the club replace the tables and chairs in the dining room and that a committee be appointed with power to purchase them at a cost not to exceed $5000."

"I move that the grounds committee be empowered to purchase concrete planters for the pool patio at a cost not to exceed the grounds committee budget."

"I move that the budget be amended to include the income from the Winter Dance and the expenses for the president to attend the regional conference." (Incidental Main Motion)

See Chart page 47.   Test Yourself, Page 85, #4.

A *Resolution* is a main motion and should be in writing. A very important motion should be in the form of a resolution. A resolution may have a preamble or not. The preamble may be a brief statement of background.

How to Write a Resolution

- A long or complicated motion should be in writing and may be in the form of a resolution. It should be written in advance if possible.

- A resolution may have two parts, the *preamble* and the *resolution*. There may be several preamble clauses and several resolving clauses in an elaborate resolution, or it may be as simple as a motion, using the word *"Resolved"* instead of the words *"I move."* It is not required to have a preamble.

- Reasons for a *motion's* adoption should not be included in the motion itself. Members may agree with the proposed action but not your reasons for it and vote against it. Such reasons within the body of an ordinary motion may be considered debate and would not be in order.

- However, the advantage of a preamble to a *resolution* is that it states the reason for the resolution, but it is considered separately. A preamble may be just a simple statement of background. When a resolution has a preamble, the preamble is not open to amendment until the resolving clauses have been debated and amended. The vote is then taken on the entire resolution, which includes the preamble.

- The negative vote is not taken on a courtesy or complimentary resolution unless a member requests that the *no* vote be taken.

- A resolution is a main motion. All rules relating to the main motion apply to a resolution.

- An elaborate resolution contains several *preamble clauses* and several *resolving clauses*. Write each clause as a separate paragraph.

- Begin each preamble paragraph with *"Whereas"* followed by a comma. The next word begins with a capital letter. The preamble, even if it contains several paragraphs, should not contain a period. Close each preamble paragraph with a semi-colon, followed by the word *"and."* Close the last preamble paragraph with a semi-colon, after which a connecting phrase such as *"therefore"* or *"therefore, be it"* or *"now, therefore, be it"* may be used. When one of these phrases is used, no punctuation should follow it and it should be placed at the end of the preamble paragraph.

Key words and phrases:
resolution
preamble
clause
paragraph

- The word *"Resolved"* is underlined, printed in Italics or upper case letters, is followed by a comma and the word "That" which begins with a capital T. Begin each resolving paragraph this way or number them after the first *"Resolved."* Close each resolving paragraph with a semi-colon, the next to last paragraph with a semi-colon, followed by the word *"and"*, and end the last resolving paragraph with a period.

Examples

Resolved, That the Bird Watchers' League provide binoculars for each Junior member.

• • • •

Whereas, Raffles are a very effective fund raiser for nonprofit organizations; and

Whereas, Currently raffles are unlawful in this State; therefore

<u>Resolved,</u> That this organization write to state legislators urging repeal of the law forbidding raffles;

<u>Resolved,</u> That such letters also urge that repeal of the law apply to nonprofit organizations only; and

<u>Resolved,</u> That this organization urge other nonprofit organizations to join us in this effort.

• • • •

RESOLVED, That this organization _____;

   2.   That such letters _____;

   3.   That this organization _____.

Test Yourself, Page 97, #17.

Subsidiary Motions

Subsidiary Motions apply to the main motion in different ways to modify it, delay action on it, or otherwise dispose of it.[1] For rules, see Chart on page 47.

Key words and phrases:
modify
delay
dispose
pending

To Postpone Indefinitely

The purpose of the motion *To Postpone Indefinitely* is to reject the main motion for the remainder of the session. This is the lowest ranking subsidiary motion. It *ranks* just above the *Main Motion*. It is not in order if anything except the main motion is pending. It opens the main motion to debate; therefore, members who have exhausted their right to speak have another opportunity to debate the main motion. Example: "I *move that the question be postponed indefinitely.*"

> Rules: it requires a second, it is debatable, it is not amendable, and it requires a majority vote to adopt.

To Amend

The motion *To Amend* ranks just above the motion *To Postpone Indefinitely* when applied to the main motion. Amendments change the wording of a motion or resolution by the following three methods: to insert or to add, to strike out, and to strike out and insert.

A. to insert words, or to add words at the end
B. to insert a paragraph, or to add a paragraph
C. to strike out words or to strike out a paragraph
D. to strike out and insert words
E. to substitute (paragraphs)

An amendment must be *germane*, that is, it must relate to the motion it is proposed to amend. An amendment may also be amended, using the methods described above. However, there can be only one primary amendment and one secondary amendment pending at the same time, and there can be no amendment to the third degree.

> Rules: it requires a second, it is debatable, it may be amended, and it requires a majority vote for adoption.

---

[1] RONR, p. 123

Example: to amend

- A main motion is pending: "That the club purchase new furniture for the clubhouse waiting room."

- A member rises, is recognized by the Chair; *"I move to amend the motion by inserting the word 'wicker' before the word 'furniture'."* Another member seconds the motion.

- The Chair: *"It is moved and seconded to amend the motion by inserting the word 'wicker' before the word 'furniture'. Is there any discussion?"* (A secondary amendment is now in order, but it must be germane to 'wicker'.)

- Member: *"I move to amend the amendment by striking out the word 'wicker' and inserting the word 'rattan'."* Another member seconds the motion.

- The Chair: *"It is moved and seconded to amend the amendment by striking out the word 'wicker' and inserting the word 'rattan'. Is there any discussion?"*

→ Now a *Main Motion,* a *Primary Amendment,* and a *Secondary Amendment* are pending. A third amendment is not in order.

- After discussion, the Chair *puts* the question: *"The question is on the motion to amend the amendment by striking out the word 'wicker' and inserting the word 'rattan'. Those in favor, say "aye." Those opposed, say "no." The "ayes" have it and the motion is adopted."*

- The Chair: *"The question is on the amendment to the main motion to insert the word 'rattan' before the word 'furniture'. Is there any discussion?"*

→ The word 'Wicker' is no longer pending; it has been struck out, and 'rattan' has taken its place.

- The Chair: *"Those in favor of amending the main motion by inserting the word 'rattan' before the word 'furniture', say "aye." Those opposed, say "no." The "ayes" have it and the amendment is adopted."*

- The Chair: *"The question is on the amended motion 'that the club purchase new rattan furniture for the clubhouse waiting room'. Is there any discussion?"**

* The motion may be further amended at this time. When the motion has been perfected by amendment, the Chair takes the vote on the **amended main motion.**

When many words are to be changed in a motion, the preferred method of amendment is *To Substitute*.

Amendment by Substitution

1. Amendment by Substitution applies to a paragraph, a series of paragraphs, or to an entire resolution.[1]
2. Amendment by substitution is a primary amendment and must be germane.
3. While the proposed substitute is pending, secondary amendments may be made to either the pending question or to the proposed substitute, but only one at a time.
4. While the substitute is pending, debate can go into the merits of both the pending question and the proposed substitute.
5. The pending question is amended first, then the proposed substitute may be amended.
6. After both the pending question and the proposed substitute are perfected by amendment, the Chair puts the question on substituting the proposed substitute for the pending question. If the amendment by substitution is adopted, the substitute becomes the *amended motion*. The original motion is no longer pending.
7. At this time, the amended motion may be amended only by adding words at the end.
8. The Chair puts the question (takes the vote) on the amended motion.

Examples: *"I move to substitute for the pending question the following: That ...."*

"I move to substitute for paragraph three of the resolution the following: ...."

"I move to substitute for the pending resolution the following resolution: ...." This motion is in order after all parts of the pending resolution have been debated and amendment is open on the entire resolution.

---

[1] RONR, p. 155

**Steps For Considering
An Amendment
By Substitution**

6. The Chair takes the vote on adoption of the Amended Main Motion.

5. The Chair reads the Main Motion as amended, and the Substitute as amended. The Chair takes the vote on whether to substitute.
If the substitute carries, it becomes the Amended Main motion.

4. The proposed Substitute may be amended (secondary amendment).

3. The Main Motion may be amended (secondary amendment).

2. A member moves to substitute another motion (primary amendment).

1. A Main Motion is pending.

To Commit or Refer

The purpose of this motion is to place a question in the hands of a standing or special committee to investigate and report back on the matter referred to it. It *ranks* just above the motion *To Amend. Debate* on the motion to commit is limited to: the appropriateness of committing the main question, instructions to the committee, and to which committee to refer the question. *Amendment* is limited to: another committee, adding instructions, and method of appointment of the committee. See Committees, page 54.

Key words and phrases:
commit
refer
limited debate
limited amendment

Rules: it requires a second, it is debatable as to the advisability of referring the main question to a committee, it is amendable as to which committee, how many members shall serve on it, and how the committee shall be appointed, and it requires a majority vote for adoption.

Examples:
"I move to refer the pending question to a committee of three appointed by the President, and that the committee report at the next meeting."

"I move that the question be referred to the Finance Committee."

To Postpone to a Certain Time

The purpose of this motion is to postpone action on a pending question to a definite day, meeting, or hour. It *ranks* just above the motion *To Commit*. Postponed questions come up under Unfinished Business and General Orders unless made a general order for a certain hour (majority vote), or a Special Order (two-thirds vote). *Debate* is limited to the merits of postponement and the suitability of the time. *Amendment* is limited as to time, and as to making a special order. *A question cannot be postponed beyond the next regular meeting.* To take up a postponed question before the specified time requires a suspension of the rules (two-thirds vote).

See general and special orders, pages 49-51.

Rules: it requires a second, it is debatable, it may be amended, and it requires a majority vote for adoption.

Examples:

"*I move to postpone consideration of the motion until the next meeting.*"

"*I move to postpone consideration of the question until four o'clock.*"

To Modify Debate

The purpose of this motion is to limit or extend the limits of debate as to time, length of speeches, or number of speeches members may make. It *ranks* just above the motion *To Postpone to a Certain Time.* This motion requires a two-thirds vote to adopt. RONR, page 382, states that a member may speak no longer than ten minutes and no more than twice on the same question on the same day. The motion *To Modify Debate* is *not debatable* and may only be *amended* as to time. Amendment of the motion requires only a majority vote, but adoption of the motion requires a two-thirds vote. *To Modify Debate* applies only to the immediately pending question, and others as specified in the motion.

Key words and phrases:
modify debate
limit
extend
debate
immediately pending
*   question*

Rules: it requires a second, it is not debatable, it is amendable, and it requires a two-thirds vote for adoption.

Examples:
"I move that debate on the question be closed and that the vote be taken at one o'clock."
"I move that debate on the pending question be limited to 12 minutes."
"I move that in debate on the pending question, members be allowed to speak only once and no longer than 5 minutes."

The Previous Question

The purpose of this motion is to close debate, to prevent further amendment, and to proceed immediately to the vote. It *ranks* just above the motion *To Modify Debate*. This motion requires a two-thirds vote for adoption. *"I move the previous question."*

A call from a member, "Question! Question!" or "I call the question!", does not automatically close debate. Debate is a right of members and cannot be denied by the demand of a single member.

The Previous Question may be called on a motion that is not debatable but is amendable. Adoption of the motion in that case prevents amendment.

The motion for the Previous Question is *not debatable.*

The Previous Question is exhausted at the adjournment of the session in which it was adopted.
'Exhausted' means that any unexecuted part of the motion is no longer in effect after a specific time.

This motion, if adopted, stops debate on the immediately pending question.

If it is desired to stop debate, for example, on a main motion with adhering motions such as amendments, the form is: *"I move the previous question on all pending questions."*

Key words and phrases:
rank
exhausted

Rules: it requires a second, it is not debatable, it is not amendable, and it requires a two-thirds vote to adopt.

To Lay the Question on the Table

The purpose of this motion is to lay aside a question *temporarily* to take up a matter of urgent business.

This the *highest ranking* of the subsidiary motions. *This motion is not debatable and cannot be qualified in any way.* It may not be amended.

This is a frequently misused motion. If the intent of the maker of the motion is to kill the motion under discussion, *To Lay The Question on The Table* is not in order, and should not be allowed by the Chair. See 'to postpone indefinitely', page 27.

"I move that the question be laid on the table." To take a question from the table, use the motion *To Take From The Table*. *"I move to take from the table the motion that ...."*

A motion laid on the table must be taken from the table by a motion of any member before the adjournment of the next regular meeting or the question dies.

Any member may make the motion *To Take From The Table.*

Subsidiary Motions[1]
See Chart p. 47.
Test Yourself, p. 88, #7.

---

[1] RONR pp. 123-216

Key words and phrases:
temporarily
misused motion
not in order

Practice Table - Subsidiary Motions

To lay the question on the table	S, M
The previous question	S, 2/3
To modify debate	S, LA, 2/3
To postpone to a certain time	S, LD, LA, M
To commit or refer to a committee	S, LD, LA, M
To amend the main motion	S, D, A, M
To postpone indefinitely	S, D, M

S -	Requires a second
LA -	Limited amendment
D -	Is debatable
M -	Majority vote to adopt
A -	Is amendable
2/3 -	2/3 vote to adopt
LD -	Limited debate

Key words and phrases:
script
indefinitely

Write a practice script using a main motion and subsidiary motions to dispose of it. Make use of all rules for the motions. Check your script with the above practice table.

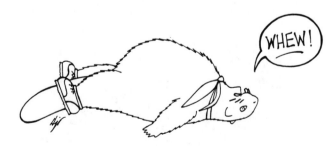

Is It Germane?

Remarks on the pending question must be *germane*.[1]

An amendment must be germane to the motion it proposes to amend.

To be germane is to involve the immediately pending question or to relate to the immediately pending subject in some way.

Key words and phrases:
germane
related
immediately pending
*   question*

Example:

A main motion is pending that *"the club purchase a gavel for the president."*

A member moves to *"amend the motion by inserting the word 'mahogany' before the word 'gavel'."*

Debate must be confined to the immediately pending question—the amendment.

Therefore, a member may not discuss the pros and cons of *purchase*, as it is not germane to *mahogany*.

After the amendment has been disposed of and discussion returns to the main motion, a remark relating to *purchase* is in order—because it is germane to the immediately pending question—the main motion.

See *To Amend,* pages 27-30.

------

1 RONR, pp. 128, 386-387 and *Parliamentary Law,* p. 19

Privileged Motions

Privileged motions are of such importance that they take precedence of all other motions. Privileged motions are not debatable. See Chart page 47.

See Chart page 47.

Key words and phrases:
privileged
demand
assembly
recess

To Call For the Orders of the Day. This is the lowest ranking of the five Privileged motions. It is used to demand that an item in the order of business be taken up. It is used when there is an obvious and unnecessary deviation from the adopted order of business or agenda. *"I call for the orders of the day."*

> Rules: it does not require a second because it is a demand by a single member, it is not debatable, it is not amendable, and requires no vote, unless there is an objection. A two-thirds vote is required to prevent proceeding to the Orders of the Day.

Questions of Privilege. These are motions relating to the safety or comfort of the *assembly*, e.g., to open a window, reduce noise, etc. *"Mister President, I rise to a question of privilege."*

> Rules: it does not require a second, it is not debatable, it is not amendable, and no vote is taken unless there is a difference of opinion on the subject of the privilege. Usually the chair handles the question by general or unanimous consent.

To Take a Recess. This provides a break in a meeting, usually for a few minutes, but it can be for longer. Examples: *"I move that we recess for 15 minutes."*; *"I move that we recess until 1:00 P.M."*

> Rules: it requires a second, it is not debatable, it may be amended, and it requires a majority vote to adopt.

To Adjourn. This motion, if adopted, officially closes the meeting. As a privileged motion, it cannot be qualified in any way. The *Chair* must declare the meeting adjourned. There are motions which can be made after the motion to adjourn is adopted and before the Chair declares the meeting adjourned.
"Madam President, I move to adjourn."

Key words and phrases:
adjourn
chair declares
general consent
continued meeting

> Rules: it requires a second, it is not debatable, it is not amendable, and it requires a majority vote to adopt. If the motion is adopted, the meeting is closed when the chair declares the meeting adjourned. When there is no motion to adjourn, the Chair may adjourn a meeting by general consent.

Steps that may be taken while the motion to adjourn is pending, and before the Chair has declared the meeting adjourned: announcements and notices, business *requiring* attention, to *make* the motion *to reconsider*, but not to *take up* reconsideration, and *to fix the time to which to adjourn.*

To Fix the Time To Which to Adjourn. This is the highest ranking of the privileged motions and of the 13 ranking motions. This motion designates another day or time to which to continue the present meeting. Example: *"I move that when we adjourn, we adjourn to meet tomorrow at three o'clock."* If adopted, this means that the present meeting will continue tomorrow at three o'clock. This motion does not adjourn a meeting. The minutes reflect that the adjourned meeting is a continuation of the present meeting.

> Rules: it requires a second, it is not debatable, it is amendable as to the date and time, and it requires a majority vote to adopt.

Practice writing a motion to *Fix the Time to Which to Adjourn*, continuing the meeting next Friday at 4:00 P.M.

Motions That Bring a Question
Again Before the Assembly

(Bring Back Motions)

To Reconsider. The motion to *Reconsider the Vote* must be made by a member who voted on the prevailing side, affirmative *or* negative. It is debatable if the motion to be reconsidered is debatable. The motion to *Reconsider the Vote* must be made on the same day as the motion to be reconsidered was made, and must be called up before the adjournment of the next regular meeting.

Key words and phrases:
majority vote
two-thirds vote
reconsider

This motion may be *made* after the motion to adjourn has been adopted, but the chair has not yet declared the meeting adjourned, although the question to be reconsidered may not be *taken up* at that time.

Reconsideration may be moved only on the same day as the vote on the motion to be reconsidered was taken, or in a session of more than one day–the same day or the next *business* day.
"I move to reconsider the vote on the motion that ...."

> Rules: it requires a second, it is debatable if the motion to be reconsidered is debatable, it may not be amended, and it requires a majority vote to adopt.
> When it is adopted, it opens the main question to debate again, before the vote is retaken.

To Take From the Table. This motion is to take from the table a motion which was laid on the table. Any member may make the motion. *"I move to take from the table the motion that ...."*

> Rules: it requires a second, it is not debatable, it is not amendable, and it requires a majority vote to adopt.
> When a question is taken from the table, debate resumes where it left off when it was laid on the table.

To Rescind. This is *an Incidental Main Motion.* The motion to Rescind is used to repeal an action that the assembly has taken previously. A vote cannot be rescinded after action has been taken, such as the signing of a contract, a resignation, etc. This motion requires a two-thirds vote, or a majority of the entire membership, or a majority vote with previous notice. *"I move to rescind the motion that ...."*

> Rules: it requires a second, it is debatable, it may be amended, and it requires a majority vote with notice or a two-thirds vote without notice.

To Discharge a Committee. The assembly takes a matter out of the hands of a committee before the committee has made a final report, and considers the subject which had been referred to the committee. *"I move to discharge the committee to which was referred the motion that ... and take up the question."*

> Rules: it requires a second, it is debatable, it is amendable, and it requires a majority vote with notice or a two-thirds vote without notice to adopt.

To Amend Something Previously Adopted. This motion can be applied to main motions, bylaws, special rules of order, and minutes of previous meetings. The vote required for adoption is the same as *To Rescind,* except in the case of amendment of the bylaws. To amend the bylaws rrquires two-thirds *and* previous notice unless the bylaws specify otherwise. *"I move to amend the previously adopted motion that ... by striking out the words ... and inserting the words ...."*

> Rules: it requires a second, it is debatable, it is amendable, and it requires a majority vote with notice or a two-thirds vote without notice to adopt.

Bring Back Motions[1]
See Chart on page 47.

Practice writing motions to rescind, to discharge a committee, and to amend something previously adopted, using motions from your organization's recent history.

Key words and phrases:
previously adopted
take up the question
minutes
without notice
previous action
rescind

---

[1] RONR, pp. 294-329

Incidental Motions

This class of motions deals with procedures arising out of: other pending motions, another motion or item of business. These motions are incidental to the business that is pending or that has been pending or will be pending. *Incidental Motions* are voted on as they arise, and most are not debatable.

Key words and phrases:
pending motion
method of voting
divide the question
divide the assembly

See Chart on page 48 for rules relating to incidental motions.[1]

Some Incidental Motions:

Method of Voting. *"I move that the vote on the motion "..." be taken by ballot."* *"I move that voting in the election be by ballot."* (This motion may be made when the bylaws do not specify the method of voting.)

> Rules: it requires a second, it is not debatable, it is amendable, and it requires a majority vote for adoption.

Division of the Question. The purpose of this motion is to divide a question which has more than one part, each part capable of standing alone as a separate motion. *"I move to divide the question."*

> Rules: it requires a second, it is not debatable, it is amendable, and it requires a majority vote to adopt.

Division of the Assembly. This is a call for a *rising* vote. *"I doubt the vote."* *"I question the vote."* *"I call for a division."* A rising vote may be demanded by a single member, without a second. The purpose is to verify a voice vote which appears to be close.

> Rules: it does not require a second because it is a demand, it is not debatable, and it is not amendable. The motion is out of order when the result of the vote is very clear without verification by rising.

On important or controversial questions, the Chair may take a *counted rising vote*, or a member may make the motion to have the vote counted. *"I move that the vote be counted."* Although the motion *Division of the Assembly* is a demand, the motion that *The Vote Be Counted* is not, and it requires a second and a majority vote to adopt.

---

[1] RONR, pp. 247-293

Withdraw a Motion. Before a motion is stated by the Chair as pending, the maker of the motion may withdraw his motion without permission of the assembly or the seconder. However, after the question has been stated by the Chair, it is in the possession of the assembly and the maker of the motion must request that the motion be withdrawn.

"I request permission to withdraw the motion." Again, permission of the seconder is not required.

Key words and phrases:
withdraw
permission
general consent
violation

> Rules: The Chair will usually withdraw a motion by general consent. If there is an objection to withdrawal, a vote must be taken on whether to permit withdrawal of the motion. In that case a majority vote will withdraw the motion.
>
> When the motion to withdraw a motion is made by another member after the request has been made by the maker, no second is required.

Point of Order. This motion should be used when there is a violation of the rules of order, bylaws, or laws of the land. Example: *"Mr. President, I rise to a point of order."* Chair: *"State your point of order."* The member raises his point, referring to the parliamentary authority, bylaws or other rules. The chair will say either *"Your point is well taken,"* and correct the procedure, or *"Your point is not well taken,"* and explain why. No other members may debate the point unless the Chair asks for information from the parliamentarian or other knowledgeable member, or the chair submits the question to the assembly for a decision.

The motion is out of order if it is used to delay the meeting or to cause disruption. It should apply to serious infractions of the rules, and not be used frivolously. A member who constantly raises points of order on minor points is a nuisance.

> Rules: no second is required, it is not debatable, it is not amendable, and the chair rules. If the chair rules the point not well taken, one member and a seconder may appeal from the decision of the chair. The assembly rules on whether to sustain the decision of the chair.

Parliamentary Inquiry. A member rises to ask a question on parliamentary procedure relating to the business of the assembly. For example: *"I rise to a parliamentary inquiry."* *"Madam President, would it be in order at this time to ...."* or *"Mr. Chairman, what vote is required to adopt the pending motion?"*

> Rules: it does not require a second because it is a request, it is not debatable, it is not amendable, and the chair answers the question.

Point of Information. A member rises to ask a question relating to the business of the assembly or a pending motion. *"Mr. President, I rise for information."* The Chair will say, *"State your question."* and the member asks his question. The question is directed to the Chair or to another member *through* the Chair, not directly from one member to another.

> Rules: it does not require a second because it is a request, it is not debatable, it is not amendable, and the chair answers the question or directs the question to another knowledgeable member.

NOTE: Incidental motions should not be confused with *Incidental Main Motions*, as they are a separate class of motions. See pages 45 and 46 for a discussion of incidental main motions.

Study the Chart of rules on page 48, then Test Yourself, page 89, #8 and page 90, #9.

Incidental Main Motions

Incidental Main Motions relate to the business of the assembly and do not introduce a new subject for consideration. See page 20.

Incidental Main Motions resemble motions of other classes, but may only be made when *no other business is pending.*

1. Incidental Main Motions which require a majority vote for adoption:

Adjourn, when *qualified,* such as, *"I move that we adjourn at five o'clock.",* or when no provision has been made for another meeting (such as the last meeting of a convention).

Adopt a committee recommendation not relating to a referred motion. When a committee chairman has reported committee recommendations, but has not moved to adopt them, any member may do so.

> Rules: it requires a second, it is amendable, it is debatable, and it requires a majority vote to adopt.

Fix the Time to Which to Adjourn, when no other business is pending. Otherwise this is a privileged motion.

> Rules: It requires a second, it is debatable, it is amendable, and it requires a majority vote to adopt.

Prescribe the Method of Nominations, when no election is pending. *"I move that in the election tomorrow morning, we nominate by ballot."*

> Rules: it requires a second, it is debatable, it is amendable, and it requires a majority vote to adopt.

Ratify emergency action taken at a meeting where there was no quorum, or to ratify an action taken outside a meeting. *"I move to ratify the action of the president taken during the emergency meeting on May 12, that the leaking roof be repaired at a cost of ...."*

> Rules: it requires a second, it is debatable, it is amendable, and it requires a majority vote to adopt.

Key words and phrases:
qualified
ratify
resemble
pending
emergency action

1. (Continued)

Recess, when no other business is pending. *"I move that we take a recess at five o'clock."*

Key words and phrases:
suspend
limit debate
objection to consideration
postpone an event

> Rules: it requires a second, it is debatable, it is amendable, and it requires a majority vote to adopt.

Suspend a standing rule for the duration of the session.

2. Incidental Main Motions which require a two-thirds vote for adoption:

Limit Debate or limit the number of times a member may speak on a question, when no question is pending. This motion requires a second, it is not debatable, it is amendable, and it requires a two-thirds vote for adoption.

3. Incidental Main Motions which require for adoption a vote of: majority with notice, or two-thirds, or a majority of the entire membership:

Amend Something Previously Adopted
Postpone an *event* or action previously adopted.
Rescind a previously adopted action.

> Rules: These motions require a second, they are debatable, they are amendable, and they require a two-thirds vote for adoption.

4. Incidental Main Motion which requires previous notice *and* two-thirds vote for adoption:

Amend the Bylaws. This is a form of the motion to amend something previously adopted. However, amendment of bylaws has special rules.

5. The motion *Objection to the consideration of the question* cannot be applied to an Incidental Main Motion.

6. It is important to remember that Incidental Main Motions which resemble other classes of motions *are in order only when no other motions are pending*. As main motions, they require a second, are debatable, amendable, and with the exceptions noted above, require a majority vote for adoption.

Incidental Main Motions[1]

Test Yourself, page 97, #18 and page 99, #21.

---

[1] RONR, pp. 66, 74, 98, 121-122, 189

Motion	Second	Debatable	Amendable	Vote	Reconsider The Vote
RANK		**Privileged Motions**			
Fix The Time To Which To Adjourn	Yes	No	Yes	Majority	No
Adjourn	Yes	No	No	Majority	No
Recess	Yes	No	Yes	Majority	No
Raise A Question Of Privilege	No	No	No	Chair rules	No
Call For The Orders Of The Day	No	No	No	Demand	No
RANK		**Subsidiary Motions**			
Lay The Question On The Table	Yes	No	No	Majority	No
Previous Question	Yes	No	No	2/3	Yes
Modify Limits of Debate	Yes	No	Yes	2/3	Yes
Postpone To A Certain Time	Yes	Yes	Yes	Majority	Yes
Refer To A Committee	Yes	Yes	Yes	Majority	Yes
Amend The Main Motion	Yes	Yes	Yes	Majority	Yes
Postpone Indefinitely	Yes	Yes	No	Majority	Aff. only
RANK		**Main Motion**			
Main Motion	Yes	Yes	Yes	Majority	Yes
Motions That Bring a Question Again Before The Assembly					
Take From the Table	Yes	No	No	Majority	No
Rescind Amend Something Previously Adopted Discharge A Committee	Yes	Yes	Yes	**	Neg. only
Reconsider	Yes	***	No	Majority	No

** Majority with notice or 2/3   *** Yes, if question to be reconsidered is.

Aff.= Affirmative

Neg.= Negative

Incidental Motions	Second	Debatable	Amendable	Vote	Reconsider The Vote
Appeal From The Decision of The Chair	Yes	1*	No	Neg. Maj.	Yes
Be Excused From A Duty	2*	Yes	Yes	Majority	Negative only
Call For A Separate Vote	No	No	No	Demand	No
Close Nominations	Yes	No	Yes	2/3	No
Close The Polls	Yes	No	Yes	2/3	No
Consider Seriatim	Yes	No	Yes	Majority	No
Count The Vote	Yes	No	Yes	Majority	No
Create A Blank	Yes	No	Yes	Majority	No
Divide The Assembly	No	No	No	Demand	No
Divide The Question	Yes	No	Yes	Majority	No
Method of Voting	Yes	No	Yes	Majority	Yes
Object To Consideration	No	No	No	**	Negative only
Point Of Order	No	No	No	***	No
Point of Information	No	No	No	No vote	No
Read A Paper	Yes	No	No	Majority	Yes
Reopen Nominations	Yes	No	Yes	Majority	Negative only
Reopen The Polls	Yes	No	Yes	Majority	Negative only
Request To Withdraw a Motion	3*	No	No	Majority	Negative only
Suspend Rules of Order	Yes	No	No	2/3	No
Suspend Standing Rules	Yes	No	No	Majority	No
Vote By Ballot	Yes	No	Yes	Majority	Yes

* Page numbers for RONR: [1] 256, [2] 291, [3] 283

** 2/3 in the negative to prevent consideration

*** Chair rules

Orders of the Day

An Order of the Day

An Order of the Day is a question *postponed to or scheduled for a certain time.* An Order of the Day cannot be taken up before the designated time except by: reconsidering the vote that postponed the question, or by a two-thirds vote in the affirmative to suspend the rules and take up the question ahead of time.[1]

See *Postpone to a Certain Time* page 32.

Key words and phrases:
order
general order
postponed
question
special order

Orders of the day are defined as two separate groups:
General Orders and **Special Orders**.

General Orders *

- When a question is postponed to a certain day or meeting, it becomes a General Order and is considered at the usual place in the order of business after Unfinished Business.

- When there are several questions postponed to a particular day or meeting, they are considered in the order that they were postponed.

- Only individual questions may be postponed. An entire class of subjects cannot be postponed. (For example, Committee Reports, or Officer Reports)

- When consideration of a question is postponed to a particular hour it becomes an Order for that hour. Items which can be considered at that time and which take precedence of the General Order are: a pending question which has not been disposed of, or a Special Order made for the same hour.

- Any General Order not taken up before adjournment is taken up under unfinished business at the next meeting. (Remember that the motion to adjourn is a privileged motion.)

* Bylaw amendments are General Orders

---
[1] RONR, pp. 182, 362

Special Orders *

A question may be postponed to a certain hour or meeting and made a Special Order by a two-thirds vote. This suspends any rules that may interfere with taking up the Special Order at the specified time, excluding privileged motions. A Special Order may interrupt pending business when the specified hour arrives.

Key words and phrases:
special order
call for the orders
of the day
the special order
requirement of bylaws

* Matters which the bylaws require to be considered at a particular meeting (such as elections) are Special Orders.

To Call For the Orders of the Day

• The motion **To Call For the Orders of the Day** is a Privileged motion which forces the assembly to conform to the adopted agenda or order of business when there is an obvious deviation from it. This is only a demand that the assembly adhere to the proper schedule.[1]

• A motion to prevent proceeding to the orders of the day requires a two-thirds vote in the negative; however, a motion may be adopted by a two-thirds vote in the affirmative to extend the time for considering the pending question before proceeding to the orders of the day.

Orders of The Day may be the same as the **Order of Business**, or agenda, when classes of subjects are taken up in a particular order.[2]

The Special Order For a Meeting

1. A question for which an entire meeting is reserved is called *The Special Order For the Meeting*. It is taken up after the reading and approval of the minutes. The Special Order for a meeting takes precedence of all other orders.[3]

2. The remainder of the order of business is taken up only after The Special Order For the Meeting has been disposed of.

Agenda

The agenda, or order of business, is sometimes called the Program, especially when it is for a particular session such as an annual meeting or a convention. A program may contain items other than the order of business. These items may include speakers, workshops, meals, and other special events.

---

[1] RONR, pp. 217-222
[2] RONR, pp. 359-361
[3] RONR, p. 366

SPECIAL MEETINGS —ORDERS
OF THE DAY

- Only business included in the call (or notice) of a Special Meeting may be considered at the Special meeting, except for minor related details.

- Such questions, one or more, as specified in the call of the meeting, are The Orders of The Day for that meeting, and no others may be considered.

- When two or more questions are specified to be considered at a special meeting[1], questions made special orders for that meeting are considered before other questions. The remaining questions become General Orders.

Key words and phrases:
special meeting
call of a meeting
questions
considered
program
general order
special order
postpone consideration

DEFINITIONS

- Order of Business: Agenda; items of business to come before the meeting.

- Orders of the Day: The program, or the business of the meeting, arranged in proper order including General Orders and Special Orders.

- General Order: A motion or item of business placed in the Order of Business without the privilege of interrupting another pending question. To make a question a General Order requires a majority vote.

- Special Order: A motion or subject assigned to a certain time, and made a Special Order by a two-thirds vote. When the designated time arrives, the Special Order interrupts and supersedes any pending business.

- The Special Order For the Meeting: A question for which an entire meeting has been reserved.

> **Examples:**
> *"I move to postpone consideration of the question until the next meeting and make it a Special Order."* (2/3 vote)
> *"I move to postpone consideration of the question until four o'clock."* (General Order, majority vote)
> *"I move to postpone consideration of the question until the next meeting."* (General Order, majority vote)

Orders of the day and related subjects are complex and require study for proficiency. Consult the index of RONR and read all sections relating to the subject and the motion to *Postpone to a Certain Time.*
Test Yourself, Page 93, #13

---

[1] RONR, p. 91

Rules of the Organization

Bylaws

The rules of an organization or club are usually contained in a single document called the Bylaws.

The bylaws specify: 1) the name of the organization, 2) the purpose of the group, 3) who the members are and the membership qualifications, as well as what, if any, dues are imposed on the members, 4) what officers there shall be and how they shall be elected and for what term, 5) when and how often the meetings shall be held, 6) the composition of an executive board if there is one and what powers it shall have, 7) committees and how they shall be appointed, 8) what the parliamentary authority (manual) shall be, and 9) how the bylaws may be amended.[1]

The bylaws must not conflict with the corporate charter if there is one, or with rules of a superior body of which the group is a chapter, or any laws of the land.[2]

Bylaws cannot be suspended unless they provide for their own suspension. Violation of the bylaws is a serious membership offense. Any action taken in violation of the bylaws is invalid (null and void).

Amendment of bylaws requires sufficient notice to members and a two-thirds vote for adoption unless the bylaws provide otherwise.

To amend the bylaws is an *incidental main motion*. It may be debated, and it may be amended. An affirmative vote on the amendment of bylaws may not be reconsidered.

Bylaw amendments go into effect as soon as adopted unless a motion is adopted to prescribe another time. The bylaws may prescribe a time for amendments to go into effect.

Amendments from the floor to a proposed amendment of the bylaws may not exceed the *scope of the notice*, that is, amendments may not make any *greater* change than provided for in the notice.

Key words and phrases:
document
parliamentary authority
rules of order
conflict
violation
suspended
notice
corporate charter

---

1 RONR, p. 564
2 RONR, p. 214

Special Rules of Order

Any rules modifying debate, or any rules that are in the nature of special rules of order (those that modify the parliamentary authority adopted by the members) require a two-thirds vote after notice for adoption. Special rules of order supersede the adopted parliamentary authority (manual) and should be printed with the bylaws. Previous notice and two-thirds vote, or a majority of the entire membership, are required to amend or suspend special rules of order[1]. See Examples page 67.

Key words and phrases:
special rules or order
standing rules
powers
previous notice
two-thirds vote
convention

Rules of order

Rules of order are contained in a parliamentary manual such as Robert's rules.

Ordinary Standing Rules

In addition to bylaws and special rules of order, the organization may choose to adopt ordinary standing rules, which are rules of an administrative nature and are semi-permanent. They may be adopted by a majority vote. To amend the standing rules requires a majority vote with notice or a two-thirds vote without notice.[2]
See Examples page 67.

Any standing rules which contain special rules of order, such as those adopted for a convention, require the same vote as special rules of order for adoption and amendment.

Other Rules

Occasionally, an organization's board of directors (or board of managers or executive board) will adopt such rules called *guidelines* or *policies*. Regardless of the title of such rules, they are not binding on the general membership unless the bylaws provide that the special body have such powers to impose them. However, boards, when appointing committees, if they have the power to appoint committees, may give instructions to the committees when they are appointed.

All rules adopted by an organization should be concise, unambiguous, and clearly written with the rights of all members in mind.
• • •
"The life of an organization depends on the legal election of its officers and the legal enactment of its bylaws." George Demeter

Test Yourself, page 92, #11 and page 105, #27.

---

[1] RONR, pp. 15, 88, 385
[2] RONR, p. 17

Committees

Committee: One or more persons, elected or appointed, to consider or investigate certain matters. 1) *Standing Committees* have a continuing existence, and 2) *Special Committees* are temporary and go out of existence when they have fulfilled their instructions and have made a final report.

Key words and phrases:
committee
with power
ex officio
quorum
chairman, chair
small boards
standing committee
boards are not
 committees

- Standing committee members may serve the same term as the officers.
- If the bylaws provide for certain standing committees, there can be no others unless the bylaws provide for other means of establishing them.
- A committee appointed "with power" has the power to act on behalf of the organization only as specifically authorized.
- If the bylaws do not specify the method of electing or appointing committees, the method can be decided by general consent or by a majority vote at the time that the committee is established.
- The power to appoint committees carries with it the power to appoint the chairmen and to fill vacancies in the committees.
- The bylaws or the assembly may give the president the power to appoint committees.
- The president is ex officio a member of committees when specified in the bylaws.
- The president, ex officio, is not counted in the quorum, but may participate in debate, make motions and vote.
- A quorum of a committee is a majority of its members.
- Sub-committees report to the committee, not to the assembly.
- The first named person to a committee serves as chairman unless the bylaws specify the method of choosing committee chairmen.
- The committee chairman may participate in debate, make motions and vote.
- Motions to limit debate are not allowed in committee.
- Very large committees, more than 12, use formal procedures.
- Boards are not considered committees, and use more formal procedures. See page 56.
- No second is required to a committee recommendation or motion, unless it is a committee of one.
- An entire committee report is not usually adopted. Only the implementation of recommendations contained in the report and moved by the reporting member should be adopted.
- To *receive* a committee report just means to hear it, nothing more.
- Ad hoc. Committees *ad hoc* are special committees, as are such groups as task groups, task forces, etc. Regardless of what they are called, committees are standing committees and special committees.
- Copies of all official correspondence should be sent to the president.

Committee Reports

Key words and phrases:
report
adopt
ad hoc
third person
receive

1. Reports are written and given in the *third person.*
2. Committee reports consist of: name, the facts found, recommendations, and signatures.
3. A written report is signed by all committee members concurring, with the chairman signing first, or, if signed only by the chairman, he writes *Chairman* after his name.
4. The reporting member of the committee, usually the chairman, reads the report and moves the adoption of any action recommended in the report.

Examples:
"The committee reports...."
"The bylaws committee reports that ...."
"By direction of the committee I move that (the recommended action) be adopted."
"By direction of the committee I move the adoption of the following resolution."

Sample committee reports, page 68.
Test Yourself, page 93, #12 and page 104, #26.

Note on reports of all kinds:
   All reports are presented in the third person singular: "the president (or your president)" reports, "the committee" reports, "the secretary" reports.

Procedure in Small Boards

Large boards, larger than twelve members, should use formal procedure just as an assembly does. Small boards, however, may use procedure that is much more informal than in an assembly but not as informal as in a committee.[1]

Small boards may adopt rules for its own procedure, deciding which of the formal and informal rules that it finds expedient.

In small boards:

- Directors are not required to obtain the floor before making motions or speaking.
- There is no need to stand before speaking as in a meeting of an assembly. This applies to the chairman as well as to the members.
- There is no limit on the number of times a member may speak in debate on a question.
- Motions to limit debate should not be used in a small board. As in a committee, the board needs to thoroughly discuss a matter of business before adoption or approval. Business could be hindered instead of facilitated if this motion is allowed.
- Discussion of a matter is allowed before a motion is made. This is very different from an assembly where debate begins only after the chair has stated the motion.
- Motions may be adopted by unanimous consent. However, if there is an objection, a formal vote must be taken.
- The chairman of the board may speak in debate without rising, and may make motions and vote on all questions.
- Procedures, other than those listed above, remain as formal as they would be in a large board or an assembly.

A small board may choose to adopt rules on a level of formality somewhere between the informal and formal procedures.

Test Yourself, page 106, #28

_____

[1]RONR, 476-478

Nominations and Elections

• The bylaws should specify how the officers and directors shall be nominated and elected and the vote required for election. If the bylaws specify that elections shall be by ballot, an election by voice vote is invalid (null and void). When the vote is by ballot, the complete tellers' report is entered in the minutes. The following procedures may be used when the bylaws do not specify the methods of nominations and elections:

Key words and phrases:
elected
vote
ballot
invalid
voice vote
nomination
nominating committee
from the floor

Usual Methods of Nominating

From the Floor:
- No recognition is required. The member rises: "I nominate Bill Cody."
- No second is required.
- A member may not make a second nomination for the same office until others who wish to nominate have had an opportunity to do so.
- A person may be nominated for more than one office.

By Committee:
- The committee should be chosen in advance and should be elected if possible.
- The president may only be a member ex officio of the nominating committee when the bylaws allow it.
- Members of the nominating committee *may* be nominated for office.
- The nominating committee report should be read in full at the meeting where the election will be held, even when the nominations have been published.
- Nominations from the floor are called for after the committee reports.
- Nominees must meet any eligibility requirements set forth in the bylaws.
- No action is taken on the nominating committee report; an election is held.

Elections

By Ballot:

- Nominations may be completed for all offices and a single ballot used. Spaces should be provided on an official printed ballot for nominations from the floor and write-ins, unless the bylaws forbid write-ins.
- A separate ballot may be prepared for each office. In that case, the election follows immediately after nominations are closed for each office. The ballots are counted and the election is announced before proceeding to the next office to be voted on.
- If a person is elected to more than one office, if the person is present, he or she chooses which office to accept. If the person is not present, the assembly should vote on which office is to be assigned, and then elect a person to fill the other office.
- If the election is by majority vote and no nominee receives a majority on the first ballot, the balloting is repeated until a nominee receives a majority. On repeated balloting, *all* nominees remain on the ballot.

Key words and phrases:
ballot
printed ballot
write-ins
office
election
repeated balloting
tellers' report
chair declares

By Voice Vote (vive voce):

- Elections may be conducted by voice vote unless the bylaws specify a ballot vote.
- When there is more than one nominee for an office, the nominees are voted on in the order that they were nominated. *The first one to receive a majority vote is elected and no votes are taken on the remaining nominees.*
- New officers take office immediately after election unless the bylaws specify otherwise.

• **Tellers' Report**: The teller reads the report in full, but the *Chair* announces the result of the vote[1]. The Chair reads the tellers' report for each office and declares who is elected, then proceeds to the next office, etc. See Examples pages 69 and 70.

Test Yourself, Page 94, #14.

---

[1] RONR, p. 410

Filling Vacancies

Vacancies in office occur for numerous reasons. Filling a vacancy requires attention to the provisions of the bylaws. If the bylaws are silent on the subject of vacancies, the following procedures should be followed.

- When a member has been elected to an office and he declines, the assembly should immediately hold an election to fill the office. If he was absent at the election and declines after the meeting, an election should be held at the next meeting to fill the office. No notice of such an election is required.[1]

- Resignations are considered *requests*[2] *to be excused from a duty,* and should be accepted by the assembly. Resignations should be in writing.

- In the case of a resignation, notice should be given that an election will be held at the next meeting to fill the office. The notice may be given in the call to meeting if the resignation occurs between meetings.[3]

- In organizations with a president-elect, the bylaws should provide for a method of electing someone to that office in the event of a vacancy. See page 63.

Test Yourself, Quiz #29, page 107

Election Committee

When the number of officers, directors, and other officers is large, or when there is a likelihood of numerous nominations from the floor, an election committee should be appointed.

- The election committee may consist entirely of tellers to count the votes when the votes are by voice or by ballot, or it may have several duties.

- The committee may be instructed to plan the election procedures, to write election rules to be adopted by the assembly, and to count the votes.

- Members from all sides of a question or election should be appointed to the election committee, so that there is no question of loyalty. The assembly must have confidence that the votes will be counted accurately and that the election will be fair and according to the rules.

Ballots
- Ballots from a contested election should not be destroyed for a time specified by the assembly or by law, usually one month. The ballots should be sealed by the election committee and stored in a safe place in case a recount is ordered by the assembly.
  If there is no likelihood of the assembly ordering a recount, the ballots may be destroyed by a motion adopted by the assembly.[4]

Test Yourself, Quiz #30, page 108

---

[1] RONR, p. 292
[2] RONR, p. 292
[3] RONR, p. 292
[4] RONR, p. 412

Minutes

- The minutes are the legal record of business transacted by an organization in meetings. Minutes should never be thrown away or be destroyed. They contain the official records and history of the organization.

- The minutes are a factual record of what was done, not a record of discussion and not the opinion of the secretary. It is very important to elect someone to the office of recording secretary who can record accurately.

- The minutes are the responsibility of the secretary, and should be signed by the secretary. In some large organizations the minutes are taken by a staff member or stenographer. That does not relieve the secretary of any responsibility for their accuracy.

- The Chair may request that long or complicated motions be in writing. Resolutions should always be in writing.

- Corrections to the minutes are written in the margin. The corrected material is never erased, but circled. The correction is dated and initialed by the secretary.

- Minutes should be written on one side of the paper only, allowing substantial margins.

- It is never too late to correct the minutes, even after many years. The motion "to amend something previously adopted" can be applied to the minutes. Care should be taken that the corrections are factual and not a change of history.

- Minutes of an *Executive Session*[1], are read and approved in Executive Session.

- The question is always on approving the minutes. The minutes are not the secretary's report, but the factual record of what was done.

- Members would be wise to listen to or read the minutes very carefully for accuracy. The minutes can be used by legal counsel in the event of later conflict or previously approved inaccuracies.

Key words and phrases:
legal record
history
factual
secretary
corrections
executive session
legal counsel
accuracy

---

[1] RONR, p. 96

Content of Minutes

1. Kind of meeting: regular, special, annual, etc.
2. Name of the assembly, organization, board or committee.
3. Date, place, and time of meeting.
4. Record the fact of the presence of the president and the secretary and who called the meeting to order.
5. Record the name of the elected temporary chairman or secretary, if there is one.
6. Record the fact of a quorum present. *Some organizations list the names of those in attendance and those absent.*
7. Record whether the minutes of the previous meeting were approved, as read or as corrected.
8. Record the name of the maker of a motion, but not necessarily the name of the seconder.
9. Record all main motions (except those withdrawn), points of order and appeals, and how disposed of—sustained or not sustained.
10. Record each subject and each motion as a separate paragraph.
11. When there is an election by ballot, the full report of the tellers is entered in the minutes. Also, include any other counted vote, number for and number against.
12. Signed:_____,
     Secretary

See Sample Minutes page 71.
Test Yourself, page 95, #15.

Duties of Officers

President

RONR states that the presiding officer of an assembly should be chosen mainly for the person's ability to preside. Presidents of today's organizations have many administrative duties beyond the duty of presiding. However, presiding should always be one of those things a president does well. The president's duties are specified in the bylaws, and if the society is incorporated there will be certain duties relating to the incorporated status.[1]

As the presiding officer of the assembly, the duties are:
1. To call the meeting to order on time. See page 13.
2. To announce the business to come before the assembly, following the order of business or agenda adopted by the assembly.
3. To recognize members who are entitled to the floor for discussion, questions, or to bring business before the assembly.
4. To state the questions brought before the assembly, to put the vote on all questions not decided by general consent, and to announce the result of the vote. Action is not complete on any business until the Chair has declared the result of the vote.
5. To maintain order, to rule on matters of parliamentary procedure, and to do so impartially.
6. To expedite business without abusing the power of the office.
7. To be thoroughly familiar with all rules of the organization— bylaws, rules of order, standing rules, etc.
8. To have on hand for quick reference: bylaws, standing rules, special rules of order, parliamentary authority, lists of committees, and agenda or order of business.

• The Chair never debates a question from the chair. He relinquishes the chair to a vice-president when he debates and remains out of the chair until the question has been resolved.[2]

• The president appoints committees as specified in the bylaws, and is a member ex officio of committees only when the bylaws provide.

Key words and phrases:
presiding officer
president
administrative duties
call meeting to order
put the vote
recognize
maintain order
result of the vote

---

[1] RONR, pp. 438-458
[2] RONR, p. 389

Vice President

The vice-presidents serve instead of the president in the absence of the president. The vice-presidents serve in this capacity in the order in which they are listed in the bylaws. The vice-president automatically fills the office of president in the event of a vacancy in that office, unless the bylaws provide otherwise. The bylaws may specify other duties for the vice-presidents.

Key words and phrases:
absence of president
vacancy
recording officer
minutes
custody of funds
audit

Secretary

The secretary is the recording officer of the organization, and is the custodian of the records. The secretary keeps accurate minutes of all meetings, and signs the minutes and other documents as required. The minutes are the responsibility of the secretary even when taken and transcribed by a staff member. The minutes are signed by the secretary who is responsible for their accuracy.
See Sample Minutes, page 71.

Treasurer

The Treasurer is entrusted with custody of the funds of the organization, keeps thorough and accurate financial records as required, and makes regular reports of disbursements and income. The treasurer disburses funds only as authorized, making a financial report to the membership annually, and submitting the financial records for audit as specified in the bylaws and as ordered by the assembly. Other duties may be specified by the bylaws. See Sample Treasurer's Report, page 72.

President Elect

If the bylaws call for a president-elect there is never an election for president. The president-elect becomes president for a full term of office at the end of the previous president's term of office. In the absence of the president, the first vice-president would preside unless the bylaws provide for the president-elect to do so. Similarly, in the event of a vacancy in the office of president, the vice-president becomes president unless the bylaws provide for the president-elect to take over the office. The bylaws should provide for filling a vacancy in the office of president-elect should one occur between elections.

Parliamentarian

The parliamentarian should be knowledgeable in parliamentary procedure for all situations in which the meeting may find itself. The parliamentarian never rules on a question. That is the duty of the Chair. The parliamentarian speaks to the assembly only when requested, and that should be seldom. The presiding officer and the parliamentarian should agree in advance on the way in which the Chair will be advised during meetings so that the consulting will be as inconspicuous as possible.

The member parliamentarian should be willing to give up the right to vote and to debate during his or her term, just as the president does, except when the vote is by ballot. If the member is not willing to do that, the position should be refused. The presiding officer must be impartial and always appear to be impartial. That can be impossible if the parliamentarian is not impartial also. If your association wishes to allow the parliamentarian to vote and to speak in debate, adopt a special rule of order which allows it.

The presiding officer may take the advice of the parliamentarian or not. The Chair rules. The parliamentarian only advises.

A professional parliamentarian should be retained for meetings such as annual meetings and conventions, and when there are many conflicts among members. A registered parliamentarian will be able to advise the organization on its rules, and to write bylaw amendments or resolutions when needed.

Written opinions based upon the organization's bylaws and parliamentary authority may be obtained from some professional parliamentarians. Some organizations retain a professional parliamentarian as election supervisor for annual meetings.

The president should interview the prospective parliamentarian personally. In order to feel at ease when the time arrives for consultation, the president must have confidence in the parliamentarian.

The professional parliamentarian will require a copy of the bylaws and other rules in sufficient time to become familiar with them. The parliamentarian will require a copy of the minutes of the previous meeting. The parliamentarian should attend board meetings before the annual meeting or convention begins.

Section Two

Examples

Examples in Section Two:
Special Rules of Order
Ordinary Standing Rules
Convention Standing Rules
Committee Reports
Tellers' Report, Tally Sheet
Minutes
Treasurer's Report
Terms Used By The Chair
Glossary
Common Errors To Avoid

Additional examples will be found in the
body of the text.

The examples in this section are very basic
and are not intended to be exhaustive.

Sample
Special Rules of Order

1. During regular meetings of the club, debate on all questions shall be limited to fifteen minutes.
2. During any meeting of the club, no member may speak more than twice nor longer than three minutes on a question without permission of the assembly.

Sample
Ordinary Standing Rules

1. Regular meetings shall be held at 10:00 A.M. the third Monday of each month.
2. The immediate past president shall be responsible for purchasing a gift, the cost of which shall not exceed $100, to be presented to the outgoing president at the installation banquet in March.
3. The club shall donate at least $500 per year to a charity to be chosen by majority vote at the January meeting.

Sample
Convention Standing Rules

1. All persons shall be registered before being admitted to any business meeting.
2. Identification badges shall be worn at all times.
3. There shall be a designated seating area for delegates.
4. All resolutions, except those contained in the report of the Executive Board, shall be referred without debate to the resolutions committee to be presented with recommendations to the convention.
5. All main motions and amendments shall be sent to the Chair in writing and signed by the maker and the seconder.
6. Debate shall be limited to two minutes for each speaker and no speaker shall speak more than twice on the same question without permission of the assembly.
7. There shall be no smoking in the meeting hall.

Sample
Committee Reports

Motion referred to a committee:
The committee to which was referred the motion "that the club purchase new furniture for the clubhouse lounge" recommends adoption of the following substitute: "That the club contract to have the lounge furniture refinished and reupholstered."

_____

Chairman

Standing Committee:
The Finance Committee reports that the club has received a donation of $500, and recommends that the funds be deposited in a savings account to be opened in the name of the club at City Bank.

_____

Chairman

NOTE: The reporting member of the committee moves the adoption of a motion to implement the committee's recommendations, after having read the report. Motions from a committee do not require a second.

Sample
Tellers' Report

For President

Number of votes cast	40
Number of votes necessary for election	21
Mr. Allman received	27
Mrs. Handy received	10
Mr. Ambler received	1
Illegal votes:	
Mrs. Dour, ineligible, received	2

For Vice-president

Number of votes cast	37
Number necessary for election	19
Mrs. Likeness received	19
Mr. Compare received	10
Mr. Coffer received	8

For Secretary, Treasurer, etc.

Signed   _____

                     _____

                     _____

                                  Tellers

NOTE: When the Tellers' Report is completed, the nominees are written into the report with the member receiving the greatest number of votes listed first, the one with the second greatest number of votes second, etc., regardless of the order of the names on the ballot or the order of their nominations.

Sample
Tellers' Report
for a motion

Number of vote cast	76
Number of votes Yes	52
Number of votes No	24

_____
_____
_____
Tellers

Sample
Tellers' Tally Sheet

For President

Mr. Allman IIII IIII IIII IIII IIII II	27
Mrs. Handy IIII IIII	10
Mr. Ambler I	1
Illegal II	2
Number of votes cast	40

NOTE:
The reporting teller *only reads* the Tellers' Report, and *does not* report who is elected. It is the duty of the Chair and only the Chair to declare who is elected.

The Tellers' Report is entered in full in the minutes.

Sample
Minutes

CALL TO ORDER	The regular meeting of the Ecology Club was called to order at 10:00 A.M. at the clubhouse, Friday, November 14, 1990, by the president, Jane Treman. The secretary was present.
QUORUM	The Chair declared a quorum present.
APPROVAL OF MINUTES	The minutes of the October 14, 1990 meeting were approved as corrected.
TREAS. REPORT	The treasurer reported a balance October 10 of $657.32; receipts, $107.00; disbursements, $52.30; and a balance November 14, $712.02.
EXEC. COMMITTEE	The secretary reported for the Executive Committee and moved adoption of the recommendation that the Treasurer be authorized to offer Professor Goodtalk an honorarium of $200 to speak at our annual meeting January 13, 1991. Motion adopted.
NEW BUSINESS	Mr. Teach moved that an educational workshop, directed by the Education Committee, be held immediately following the annual meeting and luncheon on January 13, and that the public be invited free of charge. Motion adopted.
PROGRAM	Mr. Marsh presented a slide show of the region and its environmentally sensitive areas.
ADJOURN.	The meeting was adjourned at 12:05 P.M.

_____   _____
Approved   Recording Secretary

Sample
Treasurer's Report
for a small organization

Report of the Treasurer of the
Ecology Club
November 14, 1991

Balance on hand October 10, 1991 $657.32

Receipts

Members' dues	$90.00	
Sale of books	17.00	
Total receipts		107.00
Total		764.32

Disbursements

Stationery	$15.00	
Postage	37.30	
Total disbursements		52.30

Balance on hand November 14, 1991   712.02

Total $764.32

Language of the Presiding Officer

Order of Business:

- "The meeting will come to order."

- "The secretary will read the minutes of the previous meeting."

- "Are there any corrections to the minutes?"

- "Since there are no corrections, the minutes are approved as read."

  or "Are there any further corrections to the minutes?" "There are no further corrections and the minutes are approved as corrected."

- "The next business in order is the report of the treasurer."

- "Are there any questions on the report of the treasurer?"

- "The report of the treasurer will be filed."

- "The next business in order is the report of the executive committee (or board). The secretary will report." (or chairman, if other than the presiding officer.)

- "The standing committee ... will report. Mr. Hardy, Chairman."

- "The next business in order is reports of special committees. The chair recognizes the chairman of the Spring Fling Committee, Miss Adams."

- "Under unfinished business, the question ... was unresolved at adjournment of the previous meeting. The question is on the motion "to purchase a new rug for the building entrance hall." "Is there any discussion on the motion?"

- "Is there any new business?" "Is there any further new business?"

  "It is moved and seconded that 'the club purchase new furniture for the clubhouse lounge.' Is there any discussion?" *or* "Are you ready for the question?"

- "It is moved and seconded to amend the motion by inserting the word *wicker* before the word *furniture*. Is there any discussion?"

- "The question is on the motion to amend the main motion by inserting the work *wicker* before the word *furniture*. Those in favor, say *aye.*" (*or*, "As many as are in favor, say *aye*.") Those opposed, say *no*. The *ayes* have it and the motion is adopted."

- "The question is on the amended motion that 'the club purchase new wicker furniture for the clubhouse lounge.' Is there any discussion?"

Key words and phrases:
next business in order
the question
moved and seconded
are you ready for the question

- "Those in favor, say *aye*. Those opposed, say *no*. The *ayes* have it, the motion is adopted, and we will purchase new wicker furniture for the clubhouse lounge."

- "If there is no objection, the meeting will be adjourned." (pause)

- "Since there is no objection and no further business, the meeting is adjourned." *or* "Since there is no objection and no further business, the Chair declares the meeting adjourned."

- "It is moved and seconded to adjourn. Those in favor, say *aye*. Those opposed, say *no*. The *ayes* have it and the meeting is adjourned."

Key words and phrases:
affirmative
negative
rising vote

When the vote is a two-thirds vote

- "Those voting in the affirmative will rise. Be seated. Those voting in the negative will rise. Be seated. There are two-thirds voting in the affirmative and the motion is adopted." *or* "There are less than two-thirds voting in the affirmative and the motion is lost."

  or

- "Those voting in favor of the motion will rise. Be seated. Those opposed will rise. Be seated. ...."

- *Note* A rising vote is taken on any two-thirds vote when the vote is not by ballot, and when there is a call for a "division of the assembly." Counted votes, two-thirds *or* majority, should be taken by rising instead of show of hands if the group is of any size.

Other Terms

- "State your question." "State your point of order."

- "Your point is well taken." "Your point is not well taken. The parliamentary authority specified by our bylaws provides that...."

- "The motion is not in order at this time." "The motion is out of order."

- "The member's remarks are out of order, as debate must be confined to the merits of the pending question."

- "The member will confine his remarks to the merits of the pending question." "Personal remarks are out of order."

- "At this time, the Chair feels that his active participation in debate is necessary. The Vice-president will please assume the chair."

When the Chair Votes

The Chair, if a member, may vote when the vote will affect the result—to break a tie, to create a tie, to create a two-thirds, to prevent a two-thirds. This right should rarely be exercised. The Chair, if a member, votes when the vote is by ballot, but may not vote again to affect the result.

- "23 having voted in the affirmative, and 23 in the negative, the Chair votes with the affirmative; therefore, the affirmative has it and the motion is adopted."

- "23 have voted in the affirmative and 22 in the negative, and the Chair votes with the negative; therefore, there is a tie vote and the motion is lost."

- "9 voted in the affirmative and 5 in the negative. The Chair votes with the affirmative. There are two-thirds in the affirmative, and the motion is adopted."

Other Votes

When the Previous Question has been called:

- Member: "I move the previous question."   (seconded)

- Chair: "The previous question has been called on the pending motion 'that....' Those in favor of ordering the previous question will rise. Be seated. Those opposed will rise. Be seated. There are two-thirds voting in the affirmative and the previous question is ordered. The question is on the pending motion "that...." Those in favor, say *aye*. Those opposed, say *no*. The *ayes* have it and the motion is adopted."

- Member: "I move the previous question *on all pending motions.*" (seconded)

- Chair takes a rising vote to order the previous question, and immediately takes the vote on the immediately pending motion, then on all other pending motions in the reverse order of their introduction.

- When the previous question is ordered, debate and amendment are stopped on all motions specified in the motion for the previous question[1].

---

[1] RONR, p. 195

When the Chair is in Doubt

After the chair has called for the affirmative and the negative voice votes and the vote is too close to call, the chair may take a rising vote to verify the result.

"Those in favor of the motion, say *aye*. Those opposed, say *no*. The chair is in doubt as to the result of the vote. The vote will be retaken by rising. Those voting in the affirmative will rise. Be seated. Those voting in the negative will rise. Be seated. The affirmative has it and the motion is adopted."

Nominations (By Committee)[1]

- Chair: "The next business in order is election of officers. The Nominating Committee will report. Mr. Plume."

  Nominating Committee reporting member: "The Nominating Committee submits the following nominations: ..., ..." No action is taken on the report.

- Chair: "Mr. Currier is nominated for President. Are there any nominations from the floor for the office of President?" *pause* "Mr. Ives is nominated. Are there any further nominations for the office of President?" *pause* "Since there are no further nominations, the Chair declares nominations closed for the office of President."

- The chair continues as above for all offices. *Nominations may also be closed after nominations are complete for all offices.* See pages 57-59.

---

[1] RONR, pp. 422-428

Elections (By Ballot)

Key words and phrases:
tellers
mark the ballot
tellers' report

- Before ballots are distributed, the Chair instructs the members on how to mark the ballot, or, the Chair calls upon the Chairman of Tellers (or Chairman of the Elections Committee) to instruct the members on marking and folding the ballot, and how it shall be collected.

- Chair: "The tellers will distribute the ballots." When all ballots have been distributed and time allowed for marking: "Have all voted who wish to vote?" (to be certain that all marked ballots have been collected)

- After the tellers have collected all of the ballots, including the chair's (if a member): "The Chair declares the polls closed. The tellers will retire to count the ballots[1]."

- Tellers return. The Chair calls upon the Chairman of Tellers to read the Tellers' Report. See page 69.

- Chair: "For the office of President: Number of votes cast, 36. Number necessary for election, 19. Mr. Currier received 28 votes. Mr. Ives received 8 votes. The Chair declares Mr. Currier elected President."

- Chair continues as above for all offices.

If the ballots are retained, they should be sealed into a box before they leave the hands of the tellers' committee.

---

[1] RONR, p. 409

Examples of Motions

To introduce a new subject
Main motion
> I move that the club invite Jane McClaine to speak at the October meeting.

To kill a motion for the remainder of the session
Postpone indefinitely
> I move to postpone the question indefinitely.

To change the wording of a motion
Amend
> I move to amend by striking out October and inserting September.

To delay action until more information can be accumulated
Refer to a committee
> I move to refer the motion to the Finance Committee to report at the next meeting.

To delay making a decision
To postpone to a certain time
> I move to postpone consideration of the question until the next meeting.

To limit or extend the time for discussing a motion
To limit debate
> I move to limit debate on the pending question to two minutes per person.
>
> I move that debate on the motion be limited to ten minutes.

To stop debate and amendment and have the vote taken immediately
Previous question
> I move the previous question.
> I move the previous question on all pending motions.

To lay aside a motion to take up an urgent matter
Lay on the table
> I move to lay the question on the table.

To take up the question after the emergency
Take from the table
> I move to take from the table the motion relating to the speaker for the September meeting.

To end a meeting
Adjourn
> I move to adjourn.

To continue the meeting at another time
Fix the time to which to adjourn
> I move that when we adjourn, we adjourn to meet tomorrow at nine o'clock.

Examples of Motions

To have a short intermission
Recess

> I move to recess for fifteen minutes.

To reverse action previously taken
Rescind

> I move to rescind the motion adopted in August that we purchase four filing cabinets.

To change a previously taken action
To amend something previously adopted

> I move to amend the motion adopted at the August meeting to pay the president's expenses, by adding "and the executive secretary's."

> I move to amend the budget by adding the income and expense from the Spring Fling.

> I move to amend the minutes of the February meeting to include the membership report.

To allow the assembly to vote again on a previously adopted motion.
Reconsider

> I move to reconsider the vote on the motion that we sell the four acres on the northeast corner.

To nominate a member for a committee
Nominate

> I nominate John Charles.

To change the voting method of an election
Motion relating to elections

> I move that this election be held by ballot.

To change the method of nominations
Motion relating to nominations

> I move that nominations be by ballot.

To call attention to an important error in procedure
Point of order

> Point of order!

To obtain information on a pending motion
Request

> I rise for information.

To obtain information on procedure
Request

> I rise for a parliamentary inquiry.

SOME COMMON ERRORS TO AVOID

INCORRECT ✗	CORRECT ✔
✗ "I make a motion"	✔ "I move that ...."
✗ "I want to make a motion"	✔ "I move that...."
✗ "I so move."	✔ "I move that...."
✗ "Question! Question!"	✔ "I move the previous question."
✗ "Mr. Jones statement is idiotic."	✔ "I rise to speak against (in favor of) the motion."
✗ "Jane, I move that...."	✔ "Madam President." *Wait for recognition.*
✗ Tellers declare who is elected.	✔ The Chair declares who is elected. *The teller merely reads the Tellers' Report.*
✗ Introduce the head table.	✔ Introduce those *seated* at the head table.
✗ Old Business	✔ Unfinished Business
✗ "The next order of business is...."	✔ "The next business in order is ...."
✗ "So ordered."	✔ "The motion is adopted."
✗ "Those in favor signify by saying *aye*." (redundant)	✔ "Those in favor, say *aye*."
✗ "Those opposed, same sign."	✔ "Those opposed say *no*." *'Same sign' means that you are asking them to say 'aye' when they mean 'no'.*
✗ "You are out of order."	✔ "The motion is out of order." "The motion is not in order."
✗ "Are there any corrections or additions to the minutes?" (redundant)	✔ "Are there any corrections to to the minutes?"
✗ "Are there any corrections to the Treasurer's Report?"	✔ "Are there any *questions* on the Treasurer's Report?"
✗ "Do I hear a second?"	✔ "Is there a second to the motion?"
✗ "Do we have a motion to adjourn?"	✔ "If there is no further business, a motion to adjourn is in order." "If there is no objection, the meeting will be adjourned. Since there is no objection, the meeting is adjourned."

Section Three

Quizzes

On the following quizzes:

If this is a library book, or if it is your own book and you do not wish to mark up the pages, use a separate sheet of paper to write the answers to the quizzes.

When you answer any question incorrectly, look up the correct answer on the reference page in the text of this workbook, and write in the correct answer. You may check your answers using the Answer Key on page 111.

QUIZ #1

Order of business

Place the items below into the proper sequence.

A. Reading and approval of the minutes

B. New Business

C. Call to Order

D. Adjournment

E. Reports of Officers, Boards, and Standing Committees

F. Opening exercises

G. Announcements

H. Special Orders

I. Unfinished Business and General Orders

J. Reports of Special Committees

1. __C__

2. ____

3. ____

4. ____

5. ____

6. ____

7. ____

8. ____

9. ____

10. ____

Reference: Page 14

QUIZ #2

On the questions below, circle the correct answer:

1. Which item in the order of business is listed by RONR as the first item?
    a) Call to order
    b) Reading and approval of the minutes
    c) Report of officers, boards, and standing committees

2. What are some other words that describe the order of business?
    a) agenda
    b) program
    c) both of the above

3. An agenda for an entire convention is called a:
    a) program
    b) order of business
    c) guide to events

Reference, Pages 14-15

QUIZ #3

On the questions below, circle the correct answers.

1.   How does a member obtain the floor?

a)   He rises and makes his motion.

b)   He rises to point of personal privilege

c)   He rises and addresses the chair and waits to be recognized.

2.   What are the two correct words to use at the beginning of a motion?

a)   I make a motion that

b)   I move that

c)   I recommend that

3.   Who opens the floor for debate on debatable motions?

a)   the chair

b)   the sergeant at arms

c)   the secretary

4.   Who may discuss the motion?

a)   members entitled to the floor

b)   members recognized by the chair

c)   both of the above

5.   The words that the chair uses to take the vote are:

a)   The question is on the motion that ... .
     Those in favor, say aye. Those opposed, say no.

b)   All those in favor say aye. Those opposed, same sign.

c)   All those in favor signify by saying aye.

Reference: Page 17 and Page 80

QUIZ #4

On the questions below, circle the correct answers.

1.   The Main Motion:
   a. requires a second
   b. requires a two-thirds vote for adoption
   c. cannot be amended

2.   The Main Motion:
   a. alters the wording of another motion
   b. is a proposition that something be done
   c. must be in writing

3.   A resolution is:
   a. a Subsidiary Motion
   b. a Main Motion
   c. an Incidental Motion

4.   A Main Motion may only be made when no other business is pending.   (T)   (F)

5.   A Main Motion may not be amended.   (T)   (F)

6.   A Main Motion may be debated.   (T)   (F)

7.   A Main Motion requires a majority vote for adoption.   (T)   (F)

8.   The preamble to a resolution sets forth the proposed action.   (T)   (F)

9.   A resolution may have only one preamble clause.   (T)   (F)

10.   Debate on the resolving paragraphs of a resolution takes place before the preamble may be considered.   (T)   (F)

11.   Write a simple Original Main Motion.

References: Pages 23-25

QUIZ #5

On the questions below, circle the correct answers.

1. How many ranking motions are there?
    a) twelve
    b) thirteen
    c) fourteen

2. What is the lowest ranking motion?
    a) the main motion
    b) amend the main motion
    c) postpone indefinitely

3. A motion to Lay The Question On The Table is classified as what kind of motion?
    a) a privileged motion
    b) a subsidiary motion
    c) an incidental motion

4. What is the vote required to adopt the motion To Lay On The Table?
    a) majority
    b) two-thirds
    c) plurality

5. What is the definition of "Germane"?
    a) closely related in subject matter
    b) closely related in subject matter to the immediately pending question
    c) closely related to the order of business

6. How many Subsidiary Motions are there?
    a) seven
    b) three
    c) five

7. To what motion may the motion to Postpone Indefinitely be applied?
    a) only to the main motion
    b) to any motion above it in rank
    c) only to the motion to amend

8. The motion to Refer To A Committee is a:
    a) main motion
    b) subsidiary motion
    c) privileged motion

9. To Take A Recess is a:
    a) privileged motion
    b) incidental motion
    c) subsidiary motion

References: Pages 22-39

QUIZ #6

On the questions below, circle the correct answers.

1. The motion Move the Previous Question is a:
    a)   main motion
    b)   subsidiary motion
    c)   privileged motion

2. What are the two degrees of amendment?
    a)   first and second degree
    b)   there are no restrictions on the number of amendments
    c)   all of the above

3. Which motion introduces a new subject for consideration and vote?
    a)   an amendment
    b)   an original main motion
    c)   an incidental main motion

4. What type of motion is a resolution?
    a)   a main motion
    b)   a subsidiary motion
    c)   a privileged motion

5. What is the term used to define the rank of motions?
    a)   precedence
    b)   quorum
    c)   privileged

6. What motion rejects the Main Motion for the remainder of the session?
    a)   postpone indefinitely
    b)   postpone to a certain time
    c)   second

7. What kind of motion is incidental to the business of the assembly or to its previously taken action?
    a)   an original main motion
    b)   an incidental main motion
    c)   a privileged motion

8. To Call For The Orders of The Day is a:
    a)   a privileged motion
    b)   an incidental motion
    c)   a subsidiary motion

9. How many Privileged Motions are there?
    a)   five
    b)   thirteen
    c)   seven

References: Pages 22-39

QUIZ #7

On the questions below, circle the correct answers.

1. The purpose of the motion To Postpone Indefinitely is:
   a) to reject the main motion for the remainder of the session
   b) to close debate on the main motion
   c) to postpone until the next meeting

2. The purpose of the motion To Amend is to change the wording of a motion or resolution.
   (T)   (F)

3. The purpose of Amending by Substitution is:
   a) to change a word in a motion
   b) to change several words in a motion
   c) to replace the motion with another motion

4. A substitute motion:
   a) requires a second
   b) is debatable
   c) must be germane to the motion it proposes to replace
   d) all of the above

5. The purpose of the motion To Refer to A Committee is:
   a) to kill the main motion
   b) to place the matter into the hands of a few members for research and recommendations
   c) to change the purpose of the referred motion

6. The purpose of the motion To Postpone to a Certain Time is:
   a) to take up the matter at a specific later time
   b) to kill the main motion
   c) to take up the matter next year

7. The purpose of the motion to Modify Debate is:
   a) to extend the time limits of debate
   b) to limit the time of debate
   c) to limit the number of times a member may speak on a motion
   d) any of the above

8. The purpose of the motion Previous Question is:
   a) to close debate and vote immediately
   b) to limit debate as to time
   c) to limit debate as to length of speeches

9. The purpose of the motion To Lay the Question on the Table is:
   a) to kill the main motion
   b) to limit debate
   c) to put the question aside temporarily to take up a matter of urgent business

Reference Pages 22-35

QUIZ #8

Voting Requirements

On the questions below, circle the correct letters in Column B to correspond to an answer listed in Column A.

Column A	Column B				
	1. Parliamentary inquiry	A	B	C	D
A. Majority vote	2. To consider seriatim	A	B	C	D
	3. To reopen the polls	A	B	C	D
B. Two-thirds vote	4. To request information	A	B	C	D
	5. To suspend rules of order	A	B	C	D
C. No vote	6. To call for a separate vote	A	B	C	D
	7. To close nominations	A	B	C	D
D. Demand	8. To close the polls	A	B	C	D
	9. To create a blank	A	B	C	D
	10. Division of the assembly	A	B	C	D
	11. To reopen nominations	A	B	C	D
	12. Point of information	A	B	C	D
	13. Point of order	A	B	C	D
	14. Division of the question	A	B	C	D
	15. To count the vote	A	B	C	D
	16. To vote by ballot	A	B	C	D
	17. To be excused from a duty	A	B	C	D
	18. To suspend standing rules	A	B	C	D

Reference: pages 42-44, 48

QUIZ #9

On the questions below, circle the correct letters in Column B to correspond to an answer listed in Column A.

Column A

A. Subsidiary

B. Unclassified

C. Incidental

D. Main Motion

E. Privileged

Column B

1. To reconsider	A	B	C	D
2. Main motion	A	B	C	D
3. To lay the question on the table	A	B	C	D
4. To limit or extend limits of debate	A	B	C	D
5. To take from the table	A	B	C	D
6. To raise a question of privilege	A	B	C	D
7. To close nominations	A	B	C	D
8. To call for the orders of the day	A	B	C	D
9. To order the previous question	A	B	C	D
10. Resolution	A	B	C	D
11. To withdraw a motion	A	B	C	D
12. To close nominations	A	B	C	D
13. To refer to a committee	A	B	C	D
14. To amend the main motion	A	B	C	D
15. To divide the question	A	B	C	D
16. To adjourn	A	B	C	D
17. To postpone indefinitely	A	B	C	D
18. To take a recess	A	B	C	D
19. To substitute	A	B	C	D
20. Point of order	A	B	C	D

Reference: Pages 22-41, 42-44, 47-48

QUIZ #10

On the question below, circle the correct answers.

1. A Majority vote is:
   a) more than half the votes cast
   b) one more than half
   c) more than half of those present

2. A Plurality vote is:
   a) the largest number of votes cast for a candidate or motion
   b) more than half
   c) half of those voting

3. A Unanimous vote is:
   a) no dissenting votes
   b) no objections
   c) everyone voted on the prevailing side

4. What is the result of a tie vote?
   a) the motion is defeated
   c) there is no majority
   d) both of the above

5. What constitutes a quorum, when the bylaws do not specify a quorum?
   a) a majority of the membership
   b) a majority of those present
   c) the number of members who come to a meeting

6. The object of a ballot vote is usually:
   a) secrecy
   b) to have a record of the vote
   c) to avoid confusion

7. "Putting the Question" means that the Chair:
   a) takes the vote
   b) asks for debate
   c) puts the motion on the floor for debate

8. Who announces the result of a vote?
   a) the tellers
   b) the chair
   c) the secretary

9. May the maker of a motion speak against his motion ?
   a) no
   b) yes

10. May the maker of a motion vote against his motion?
   a) no
   b) yes

11. If a motion which requires a second is adopted but has not been seconded, is it a legally adopted motion?
   a) yes
   b) no

12. Define two-thirds vote.
   a) two-thirds of those present
   b) two-thirds of those voting
   c) two-thirds of the tellers

Reference: Page 18

QUIZ #11

On the questions below, circle the correct answers.

1. Which document usually contains the major rules of the organization?
    a) the minutes
    b) the standing rules
    c) the bylaws

2. When the bylaws are silent on the subject, what are the requirements for amending the bylaws?
    a) two-thirds vote
    b) two-thirds vote with notice
    c) majority vote

3. Rules which modify debate or modify the parliamentary authority are called:
    a) special rules of order
    b) standing rules
    c) standard operating procedures

4. Rules of an administrative nature are called:
    a) standing rules
    b) special rules of order
    c) bylaws

5. When may a board impose rules on the membership?
    a) anytime
    b) when the bylaws give the board the authority
    c) when the board is in session

6. May the bylaws be suspended?
    a) yes
    b) no

7. Action taken in violation of the bylaws is:
    a) a serious offense
    b) null and void
    c) both of the above

8. Other than the bylaws, which class of rules supersedes the parliamentary authority?
    a) special rules of order
    b) standing rules

9. Which rules are semi-permanent and can be amended by a two-thirds vote without notice?
    a) ordinary standing rules
    b) special rules of order
    c) bylaws

Reference: Pages 52-53

QUIZ #12

On the questions below, circle the correct answers.

1. Ordinary committees are:
   a. standing and special
   b. nominating committees
   c. sub-committees

2. Sub-committees report to:
   a. the president
   b. the assembly
   c. the committee

3. Motions not allowed in committee are:
   a. main motions
   b. modify and close debate
   c. incidental motion

4. The quorum of a committee is:
   a. two-thirds
   b. a majority
   c. those who show up

5. Vacancies in committees are filled by:
   a. the president
   b. the appointing power
   c. the committee chairman

6. Reports of committees should be written in:
   a. the third person
   b. the first person
   c. either way

Reference pages 54-55

QUIZ #13

On the questions below, circle true (T) or false (F).

1. The two groups of Orders of the Day are General Orders and Special Orders   (T) (F)

2. To make a General Order requires a majority vote.   (T) (F)

3. To make a Special Order requires a two-thirds vote.   (T) (F)

4. An entire meeting may be reserved for *the special order for the meeting.*   (T) (F)

5. General Orders may interrupt a pending question.   (T) (F)

6. When a matter is postponed to a certain hour, it becomes an Order for that hour.   (T) (F)

7. Special Orders may interrupt pending business.   (T) (F)

8. Orders of the Day may be the same as the Order of Business.   (T) (F)

9. A special meeting may only consider questions which were included in the call to meeting.   (T) (F)

Reference pages 49-51

QUIZ #14

On the questions below, circle true (T) or false (F).

1. A person may not be nominated or elected to more than one office.   (T) (F)

2. The complete tellers' report is entered in the minutes.   (T) (F)

3. No recognition is required to make a nomination from the floor.   (T) (F)

4. Nominations must be seconded.   (T) (F)

5. The president is always a member ex officio of the nominating committee.   (T) (F)

6. Members of the nominating committee may be nominated for office.   (T) (F)

7. Members must be eligible for an office to be elected.   (T) (F)

8 The Chair announces who is elected.   (T) (F)

9. If the bylaws specify a ballot vote and there is only one nominee for an office, the election may be by voice vote.   (T) (F)

10. Newly elected officers take office immediately when the bylaws do not specify a later time.   (T) (F)

11. A member may make as many nominations at one time as he wishes.   (T) (F)

12. The bylaws should specify how officers and directors shall be elected.   (T) (F)

13. On repeated balloting, only the two nominees receiving the greatest number of votes remain on the ballot.   (T) (F)

14. When the vote is by voice, all nominees must be voted on.   (T) (F)

15. A separate ballot must be prepared for each office.   (T) (F)

Reference: Pages 57-58

QUIZ #15

On the following questions, circle true (T) or false (F).

1. Minutes are the legal record of business transacted in a meeting. (T) (F)
2. Minutes are always signed by the president. (T) (F)
3. The minutes are the responsibility of the secretary. (T) (F)
4. Corrections to the minutes are made by erasing the mistakes. (T) (F)
5. Minutes may be corrected only at the next regular meeting. (T) (F)
6. Minutes of an *executive session* are read and approved only in executive session. (T) (F)
7. The minutes are the secretary's report. (T) (F)
8. It is never too late to amend previously approved minutes. (T) (F)
9. The minutes should record:
   a. the kind of meeting (T) (F)
   b. the name of the assembly (T) (F)
   c. the place and time of the meeting (T) (F)
   d. that the president was present or absent (T) (F)
   e. who presided if the president was absent (T) (F)
   f. that a quorum was present (T) (F)
   g. Mr. Adam's opinion on the motion (T) (F)
   h. the secretary's opinion (T) (F)
   i. the name of the maker of the motion (T) (F)
   j. the name of the seconder (T) (F)
   k. It is not necessary to include the tellers report in the minutes (T) (F)

Reference Pages 60-61

QUIZ #16

Glossary
Place the correct letter from Column B in the spaces in Column A.

Column A   Column B

_____ 1. Ex officio   A. Introduction to a resolution

_____ 2. Assembly   B. A ruling

_____ 3. Adopted   C. Voice vote

_____ 4. Decision   D. Section by section

_____ 5. Decorum   E. By virtue of office

_____ 6. Preamble   F. Members present at a meeting

_____ 7. Seriatim   G. Largest number of votes cast

_____ 8. Vive Voce   H. Decency of conduct

_____ 9. Plurality   I. Adopted

_____10. Receive   J. Program

_____11. Pending   K. Hear a report

_____12. Debate   L. Discussion

_____13. Germane   M. Undecided, unresolved

_____14. Agenda   N. Pertinent, closely related

_____15. Quorum   O. Number required to be present
                                     for actions taken to be legal.

_____16. Chair   P. Take the vote

_____17. Put the question   Q. Hear a report

_____18. Adjournment   R. Presiding officer

_____19. General consent   S. Close of a meeting

_____20. Receive a report   T. Written parliamentary rules

_____21. Rules of order   U. Rank

_____22. Precedence   V. No objection

_____23. Standing Rules   W. Temporarily

_____24. Speaker   X. Administrative rules

_____25. Pro tempore   Y. The member who has the
                                     floor

References: Pages 117-121

QUIZ #18

On questions 1 through 5, circle the correct answers.

1. An Incidental Main Motion relates to the business of the assembly.   (T) (F)

2. An Incidental Main Motion may be made only when no other
   business is pending.   (T) (F)

3. An Incidental Main Motion introduces a new subject for consideration. (T) (F)

4. Incidental Main Motions and Incidental Motions are the same class of motions. (T) (F)

5. The motion "Object to Consideration" may be applied to
   Incidental Main Motions.   (T) (F)

6. In Column A, circle the correct answer from Column B.

Column A   Column B

A B C D   1. Limit debate for duration of session   A. Majority with notice or two-
                                                          thirds, or majority of entire
A B C D   2. Amend bylaws   membership

A B C D   3. Postpone an event or action   B. Majority

A B C D   4. Rescind   C. Two-thirds

A B C D   5. Ratify   D. Notice and two-thirds

A B C D   6. Adjourn, when qualified

Reference: Pages 45-46

QUIZ #17

Write a resolution containing two preamble clauses and two resolving clauses.
 (Use a separate sheet of paper)

Reference: pages 25-26

QUIZ #19

General Knowledge quiz

On the questions below, circle the correct answers.

1. An *ad hoc* committee is:
    a) a temporary committee
    b) a special committee
    c) both of the above

2. What is an invalid motion or action?
    a) one that is contrary to the bylaws
    b) an illegal one
    c) one that is null and void
    d) all of the above

3. Define Decision of the Chair.
    a) the ruling of the parliamentarian
    b) a ruling by the chair
    c) an adopted motion

4. What does the word 'germane' mean when applied to an amendment?
    a) closely related to the subject being amended
    b) not in order
    c) related to the motion just adopted

5. Who, in a business meeting, is the 'speaker'?
    a) the chair
    b) the member who has the floor

6. May a member yield his time in debate to another member for the purpose of debate?
    a) Yes   b) No

7. May a person be elected as an Honorary member when the bylaws do not provide for such an office or position?
    a) Yes   b) No

8. Define "putting the question."
    a) taking the vote
    b) announcing the vote

QUIZ #20

General Knowledge Quiz
On the following questions, circle the correct answers.

1. An original main motion introduces a new subject for consideration. (T) (F)

2. An incidental main motion does not introduce a new subject for consideration. (T) (F)

3. Subsidiary motions assist the assembly in disposing of the main motion. (T) (F)

4. Privileged motions are privileged because they relate to matters of special or immediate importance. (T) (F)

5. Incidental motions relate to the pending business in some way. (T) (F)

6. Bring back motions bring a question again before the assembly for consideration. (T) (F)

QUIZ #21

The following questions relate to incidental main motions. Some incidental main motions resemble motions of other classes.

Write your answers on a separate sheet of paper.
1. When is the motion *to adjourn* an incidental main motion instead of a privileged motion?

2. What are four basic rules for the motion *to recess* when it is an incidental main motion?

3. Do these rules apply to all other incidental main motions?

4. What is the major condition for a motion of another class to become an incidental main motion?

5. What is the purpose of the motion *to adjourn* when it is an incidental main motion?

6. What vote does the motion *to limit debate* require:
    When it is a subsidiary motion?
    When it is an incidental main motion?

7. May consideration of an incidental main motion be objected to?

8. To *amend the bylaws* is an incidental main motion. What special rules apply to this motion when the bylaws are silent on the subject?

Reference pages 45-46

QUIZ #22

General Knowledge Quiz
On the following questions, circle the correct answers.

1. The main motion, the subsidiary motions, and the privileged motions may be brought to the assembly for consideration in order of their precedence, or rank to each other.   (T) (F)

2. A motion takes precedence of motions that rank below it.   (T) (F)

3. Incidental motions have no rank among themselves.   (T) (F)

4. Incidental motions are handled immediately and rank above any other motions that are pending.   (T) (F)

5. The lowest ranking motion is the main motion.   (T) (F)

QUIZ #23

General knowledge Quiz
On the questions below, circle the correct answers.

1. A Main motion may be made only when no other business is pending.   (T) (F)

2. A Main motion may be amended.   (T) (F)

3. General consent is the same as unanimous consent.   (T) (F)

4. The Chair announces who is elected.   (T) (F)

5. Putting the question means taking the vote.   (T) (F)

6. To make a General Order requires a 2/3 vote.   (T) (F)

7. Motions to limit debate are not allowed in committee meetings.   (T) (F)

8. Reports should be written in the first person singular.   (T) (F)

9. Sub-committees report to the assembly.   (T) (F)

10. Special orders may interrupt pending business.   (T) (F)

11. A quorum of a committee is a majority of the committee.   (T) (F)

12. The president, when ex officio a member of a committee, is

    counted in the quorum.   (T) (F)

13. The bylaws may be suspended at any time.   (T) (F)

14. A tie vote loses the motion.   (T) (F)

15. The maker of a motion may speak against it.   (T) (F)

16. The maker of a motion may vote against it.   (T) (F)

17. 'To Close Nominations' is an incidental motion.   (T) (F)

18. 'To postpone indefinitely' is an incidental motion.   (T) (F)

19. To Substitute is a form of amendment.   (T) (F)

20. A resolution is a main motion.   (T) (F)

21. A quorum is a majority of the members when the bylaws do not define

    the quorum for membership meetings.   (T) (F)

22. A second always means that the seconder agrees with the motion.   (T) (F)

23. A motion that is adopted is not a legally adopted motion unless it

    was seconded.   (T) (F)

24. The only business that may be transacted when there is no quorum is:
    a. Fix the time to which to adjourn   c. Take measures to obtain a quorum
    b. Adjourn   d. Recess
                                            e. All of the above

QUIZ #24

General Knowledge Quiz
On the following questions, circle the correct answers.

1. Four purposes of parliamentary procedure are: orderly conduct of business, decorum in debate, protection of members rights, and to provide a foundation for resolving disputes. (T) (F)

2. Five principles of parliamentary law and procedure are: the rule of the majority, right of the minority to be heard, equality of opinion, protection of absentees, and one subject at a time. (T) (F)

3. A point of order may be raised after a meeting if a member discovers that the chair had allowed debate on an undebatable motion during the meeting. (T) (F)

4. Decorum is simply good manners. (T) (F)

5. In debate, members may address their remarks directly to the maker of the motion. (T) (F)

6. Debate is always on the pending question. (T) (F)

7. A temporary presiding officer is addressed as Mr. or Madam Chairman. (T) (F)

8. A vice-president presiding should be addressed as Mr. or Madam President unless the president is in the room; then is addressed as Mr. or Madam Chairman. (T) (F)

QUIZ #25

General Knowledge Quiz
On the following questions, circle the
correct answers.

1. Which of the following motions
   requires a two-thirds vote?
   a) to refer to a committee
   b) to postpone indefinitely
   c) to limit debate
   d) none of the above

2. Which of the following motions
   requires previous notice and a two-
   thirds vote?
   a) to call for the orders of the day
   b) to amend standing rules
   c) to amend the bylaws
   d) none of the above

3. Which of the following motions do
   not require a second?
   a) to call for the orders of the day
   b) to make a point of order
   c) to divide the assembly (division)
   d) All of the above

4. Which of the following motions are
   Incidental Motions?
   a) to call for the orders of the day
   b) to adjourn
   c) to raise a question of privilege
   d) none of the above

5. Which of the following questions is
   adopted by a tie vote?
   a) to refer to a committee
   b) to appeal the decision of the chair
   c) to sustain the decision of the chair
   d) none of the above

6. Which of the following motions may not be
   amended?
   a) to appeal from the decision of the chair
   b) to refer to a committee
   c) to limit debate
   d) none of the above

7. Which of the following motions are not
   debatable?
   a) to limit debate
   b) to recess
   c) to fix the time to which to adjourn
   d) all of the above

8. Which of the following motions are not
   debatable and not amendable?
   a) to call for the orders of the day
   b) to lay the question on the table
   c) to raise a point of order
   d) all of the above

9. Which of the following phrases is correct
   when making a motion?
   a) I move that...
   b) I make a motion to...
   c) I recommend that...
   d) none of the above

10. Which of the following motions require only
    a majority vote?
    a) to amend the main motion
    b) to amend the amendment
    c) to lay the question on the table
    d) all of the above

QUIZ #26

On the following questions, circle the correct answers.

1. What constitutes a quorum in a committee?
   a) a majority of the members of the committee
   b) the chairman plus one-half of the members
   c) one-third of the members of the committee
   d) none of the above

2. Vacancies in a committee are filled by:
   a) the president
   b) the committee chairman
   c) the appointing power
   d) all of the above

3. Which of the following motions is not allowed in a committee?
   a) to limit debate
   b) to amend a main motion
   c) to postpone consideration until the next meeting
   d) none of the above

4. The president is ex officio a member of all committees:
   a) never
   b) always
   c) when the bylaws say so
   d) all of the above

5. An ad hoc committee is:
   a) a special committee
   b) a standing committee
   c) board committee
   d) none of the above

6. The minimum number of persons who may serve on a committee is:
   a) three
   b) one
   c) five
   d) none of the above

7. A special committee ceases to exist:
   a) when it makes a report
   b) when it makes its final report
   c) at the next regular meeting
   d) none of the above

8. If the chairman of a committee fails to call a meeting:
   a) any committee member may do so
   b) the president may do so
   c) the committee is discharged
   d) none of the above

9. When the bylaws do not specify how appointments will be made, a special committee chairman is:
   a) the first named to the committee
   b) appointed by the committee
   c) appointed by the president
   d) none of the above

Reference: pages 54-55

QUIZ #27

On the following questions, circle the correct answers.

1. The bylaws may not conflict with:
    a) the corporate charter if there is one
    b) rules of a superior body
    c) state and local laws
    d) all of the above

2. The bylaws may provide for their own:
    a) amendment by a majority vote
    b) amendment by unanimous consent
    c) amendment by the board
    d) any or all of the above

3. A motion to amend the bylaws is:
    a) a subsidiary motion
    b) an incidental main motion
    c) a privileged motion
    d) none of the above

4. Amendments from the floor to proposed bylaw amendments:
    a) may not make any greater change than provided for in the notice
    b) are primary amendments
    c) may be amended
    d) all of the above

5. Motions that are adopted that are in violation of the bylaws:
    a) are recorded in the minutes
    b) are null and void
    c) change the bylaws
    d) none of the above

6. Amendment of standing rules requires a vote of:
    a) a majority with notice or two-thirds
    b) a majority of those present and voting
    c) two-thirds with previous notice
    d) none of the above

7. Special rules of order:
    a) require a two-thirds vote to adopt
    b) may be amended by previous notice and two-thirds
    c) may be amended by a majority of the entire membership
    d) all of the above

8. The board of directors may adopt rules that are binding on the membership when:
    a) the bylaws give that authority
    b) anytime
    c) in board meetings where a quorum is present
    d) all of the above

9. The bylaws should provide for:
    a) the method of election of officers
    b) how committees shall be appointed
    c) membership qualifications
    d) all of the above

Reference: pages 52-53

QUIZ #28

SMALL BOARDS

On the questions below, circle the correct answer.

In a small board:

1. Directors must be recognized by the chair before speaking.   (T)   (F)

2. The chairman must stand while addressing the board.   (T)   (F)

3. No discussion is allowed until the chair has stated the motion
    and opened the floor for debate.   (T)   (F)

4. Motions may be adopted by unanimous consent.   (T)   (F)

5. The chairman may not speak in debate on a motion.   (T)   (F)

6. The chairman may make motions and vote on all questions.   (T)   (F)

7. There is no limit on the number of times a member may speak
    in debate.   (T)   (F)

8. All board members may remain seated during debate.   (T)   (F)

9. Motions to limit debate should not be entertained.   (T)   (F)

10. A small board is one which has no more than twelve members.   (T)   (F)

11. Larger boards (more than twelve members) use formal procedure.   (T)   (F)

Reference page 56

QUIZ #29

On the following questions, circle true (T) or false (F)

1. A member may decline an election if he is elected to an office at a meeting when he was absent.   (T) (F)

2. A member may decline an election if he is elected to an office at a meeting when he was present.   (T) (F)

3. If a member declines after an election when he was present, the assembly should immediately elect someone else to fill the office.   (T) (F)

4. Resignations are considered "requests to be excused from a duty."   (T) (F)

5. If a member resigns during his term of office, there is no need to give notice that an election will be held to fill the office.   (T) (F)

6. If a member was absent when he was elected to an office and declines, notice is required to hold an election to fill the office.   (T) (F)

Reference: page 59

QUIZ #30

On the questions below, circle true (T) or false (F).

1. An election committee may consist of only the tellers to
    count the votes.   (T) (F)

2. An election committee may have numerous duties
    related to the election and counting of the votes.   (T) (F)

3. Ballots from a contested election may be destroyed
    immediately by the tellers.   (T) (F)

4. Destruction of the ballots may be ordered by the
    assembly.   (T) (F)

Reference: page 59

On the following question, write your answer on a separate sheet of paper.
If you are working in class, pass around your answer for others to correct.

5. Write a complete tellers report for and election by majority vote:
    170 votes cast, Mr. Jones received 20, Miss Adams received 87,
    Mrs. Beam recieved 5, Mr. Dobbs received 56, and there were
    2 illegal votes for Mr. Allen who was not eligible for office.

Reference: pages 69-70

QUIZ #31

Intermediate—Problems to solve

Solve the following problems on a separate sheet of paper.

1. Write a script using correct parliamentary language, beginning with the chair's introduction of New Business, and include the following items. Include all dialogue.
    a. a main motion and a second
    b. a primary amendment
    c. a secondary amendment
    d. voting on the above motions
    e. End with the chair asking "Is there any further New Business?"

2. Write the dialogue, *in proper order,* for introducing and disposing of the following items of business.
    a. a main motion
    b. limit debate
    c. an amendment
    d. refer to a committee
    e. taking the vote

3. Write the dialogue for the following in order:
    a. a main motion
    b. a primary amendment adopted
    c. a secondary amendment defeated
    d. taking the vote

4. Write the dialogue for the chair to cast the vote to affect the outcome on a two-thirds vote when there are 75 votes cast, 50 in the affirmative, and 25 in the negative.

QUIZ #32   Review

On the following questions, circle true (T) or false (F).

1. The first item listed in the order of business by RONR is reading
    and approval of the minutes.   (T) (F)
2. A member obtains the floor by calling out "Madam President."   (T) (F)
3. A resolution is a main motion.   (T) (F)
4. The ranking motions are: main motion, subsidiary motions
    and privileged motions.   (T) (F)
5. There are seven privileged motion.   (T) (F)
6. To close the polls requires a majority vote.   (T) (F)
7. To reopen nominations requires a majority vote.   (T) (F)
8. To order the previous question is a subsidiary motion.   (T) (F)
9. To recess is a privileged motion.   (T) (F)
10. A majority vote is one more than half.   (T) (F)
11. The maker may not speak against his own motion.   (T) (F)
12. Rules which modify debate for an entire session are called
    special rules of order.   (T) (F)
13. Ordinary committees are standing committees and special committees. (T) (F)
14. The quorum of a committee is a majority.   (T) (F)
15. To make a general order requires a majority vote.   (T) (F)
16. A person may not be elected to more than one office.   (T) (F)
17. Members of the nominating committee may not be nominated for office. (T) (F)
18. The bylaws should specify how officers shall be elected and by what vote.(T) (F)
19. Debate is always on the immediately pending question.   (T) (F)
20. A motion takes precedence of motions that rank below it.   (T) (F)
21. A main motion may be amended.   (T) (F)
22. An incidental main motion may not be amended.   (T) (F)
23. Incidental motions must be germane to the pending question.   (T) (F)
24. An ad hoc committee is a special committee.   (T) (F)
25. An invalid motion is one that is null and void.   (T) (F)
26. An incidental main motion relates to the business of the assembly. (T) (F)
27. A resolution is required to have a preamble.   (T) (F)
28. A motion to *fix the time to which to adjourn* adjourns the meeting. (T) (F)
29. Use of parliamentary procedure protects the rights of the minority. (T) (F)
30. All members should know parliamentary procedure.   (T) (F)

ANSWER KEY - Quizzes 1 -

QUIZ # 1

1. C	5. J	8. B
2. F	6. H	9. G
3. A	7. I	10. D
4. E		

QUIZ # 2

1. b   2. c   3. a

QUIZ # 3

1. (c) He rises, addresses the chair, and waits to be recognized.
2. (b) "I move...."
3. (a) The chair
4. (b) Members who have been granted the floor
5. (a) "Those in favor, say *aye*. Those opposed, say *no*."

QUIZ # 4

1. A	6. T
2. B	7. T
3. B	8. F
4. T	9. F
5. F	10. T

11. Check your answer with the examples on page 24.

QUIZ # 5

1. (b) 13
2. (a) Main motion
3. (b) Subsidiary
4. (a) Majority
5. (b) Closely related, pertinent
6. (a) Seven
7. (a) Main motion
8. (b) Subsidiary
9. (a) Privileged

QUIZ # 6

1. (b) Subsidiary
2. (a) 1st & 2nd degree, primary & secondary
3. (b) Original main motion
4. (a) Main motion
5. (a) Precedence
6. (a) Postpone indefinitely
7. (b) Incidental main motion
8. (a) Privileged motion
9. (a) Five

QUIZ # 7

1. a	6. a
2. T	7. d
3. c	8. a
4. d	9. c
5. b	

QUIZ # 8

1. C	7. B	13. C
2. A	8. B	14. A
3. A	9. A	15. A
4. C	10. D	16. A
5. B	11. A	17. A
6. D	12. C	18. A

QUIZ # 9

1. B	11. C
2. D	12. C
3. A	13. A
4. A	14. A
5. B	15. C
6. E	16. E
7. C	17. A
8. E	18. E
9. A	19. A
10. D	20. C

QUIZ # 10

1. (a) More than half the votes cast
2. (a) The largest number of votes cast
3. (a) No dissenting votes
4. (a) The motion is defeated
5. (a) A majority of the members
6. (a) Secrecy
7. (a) Takes the vote
8. (b) The Chair
9. (a) No
10. (b) Yes
11. (a) Yes
12. (b) At least two thirds of the votes cast

QUIZ # 11

1. (c) Bylaws
2. (b) Previous notice and two-thirds vote
3. (a) Special rules of order
4. (a) Standing rules
5. (b) Only when the bylaws give that power
6. (b) No, unless they provide for their own suspension
7. (b) Null and void
8. (a) Special rules of order
9. (a) Standing rules

QUIZ # 12

1. A	4. B
2. C	5. B
3. B	6. A

QUIZ # 13

1. T	6. T
2. T	7. T
3. T	8. T
4. T	9. T
5. F	

QUIZ # 14

1. F	9. F
2. T	10. T
3. T	11. F
4. F	12. T
5. F	13. F
6. T	14. F
7. T	15. F
8. T	

QUIZ # 15

1. T		9. a.	T
2. F		b.	T
3. T		c.	T
4. F		d.	T
5. F		e.	T
6. T		f.	T
7. F		g.	F
8. T		h.	F
		i.	T
		j.	F
		k.	F

QUIZ # 16

1. E	15. O
2. F	16. R
3. I	17. P
4. B	18. S
5. H	19. V
6. A	20. Q
7. D	21. T
8. C	22. U
9. G	23. X
10. K	24. Y
11. M	25. W
12. L	
13. L	
14. J	

QUIZ # 17

After you have completed your resolution, compare your answer to the examples on page 26.

QUIZ # 18

1. T		6. 1.	C
2. T		2.	D
3. F		3.	A
4. F		4.	A
5. F		5.	B
		6.	B

QUIZ # 19

1. (c) A special committee
2. (d) An illegal one. Null and void
3. (b) A ruling by the chair
4. (a) Closely related to the subject being amended
5. (b) The person who has the floor
6. (b) No. The right of the floor for debate is not transferable.
7. (b) No
8. (a)

QUIZ # 20

1. T
2. T
3. T
4. T
5. T
6. T

QUIZ # 21

1. When it is qualified

2. a. It requires a second.
    b. It is debatable.
    c. It is amendable.
    d. It requires a majority vote to adopt.
3. No
4. When no other business is pending
5. To qualify it. See page 41.
6. 2/3, 2/3
7. No
8. Previous notice and two-thirds vote

QUIZ # 22

1. T
2. T
3. T
4. T
5. T

QUIZ # 23

1.	T	13.	F
2.	T	14.	T
3.	T	15.	F
4.	T	16.	T
5.	T	17.	T
6.	F	18.	F
7.	T	19.	T
8.	F	20.	T
9.	F	21.	T
10.	T	22.	F
11.	T	23.	F
12.	F	24.	e.

QUIZ #24

1. T
2. T
3. F
4. T
5. F
6. T
7. T
8. T

QUIZ # 25

1. c
2. c
3. d
4. d
5. c
6. a
7. d
8. d
9. a
10. d

QUIZ # 26

1.	a	6.	b
2.	c	7.	b
3.	a	8.	a
4.	c	9.	a
5.	a		

QUIZ # 27

1. d
2. d
3. b
4. d
5. b
6. a
7. d
8. a
9. d

QUIZ # 28

1. F
2. F
3. F
4. T
5. F
6. T
7. T
8. F
9. T
10. T

QUIZ # 29

1. T
2. T
3. T
4. T
5. F
6. F

QUIZ # 30

1. T
2. T
3. F
4. T
5. Check the accuracy of your report by referring to pages 69 and 70.

QUIZ # 31

Check your scripts with Language of the Presiding Officer, page 73, and parts of the text dealing with each subject.

QUIZ # 32 Review

1.	T	16.	F
2.	F	17.	F
3.	T	18.	T
4.	T	19.	T
5.	F	20.	T
6.	F	21.	T
7.	T	22.	F
8.	T	23.	F
9.	T	24.	T
10.	F	25.	T
11.	T	26.	T
12.	T	27.	F
13.	T	28.	F
14.	T	29.	T
15.	T	30.	T

Glossary

Ad hoc committee • A special committee.

Address the chair • To speak to the presiding officer, using the appropriate title, and asking to be recognized by the Chair to make a motion or to speak in debate.

Adjourn • Adoption of this motion officially closes a meeting.

Adjourn sine die • To adjourn without providing for another meeting, usually at the end of a convention of delegates.

Adjourned meeting • A continuation of a regular or special meeting at a later date.

Adopt • A motion is adopted when the affirmative vote prevails. A motion is lost when the negative vote prevails.

Agenda • Program. List of items of business to come before the assembly. A list of things to do. Order of business which includes call to order and adjournment.

Alternate • A member appointed or elected to take the place of another, such as a convention delegate.

Amend • To change the wording of a motion.

Amendment • A motion which alters a pending motion. (Only two amendments may be pending at one time, a Primary amendment and a Secondary amendment.) To amend the bylaws is an incidental main motion.

Announcing the vote • A statement by the Chair giving the result of a vote. Action is not complete on a motion until the Chair has announced the result of the vote.

Articles of Incorporation • Corporate Charter. A certificate issued by the state under authority of law creating an entity which may own and sell property, sue and be sued, etc. The individual members of the corporation are not liable for the debts of the corporation. There are business corporations and not for profit corporations, and each will have statutes governing them.

Assembly • Members present at a meeting.

Aye vote • The affirmative vote.

Ballot • Usually a written vote. Usually a secret vote.

Board • Board of Directors, Trustees, Managers. A group of members elected to act for the organization as specified in the bylaws.

Bylaws • A document, adopted by the organization, containing the basic rules for governing the group.

Call to order • The official opening of a meeting.

Adopted • The same as *carried.*

Chair • The presiding officer, or the station from which he presides. Mr. Chairman, Madam Chairman. The presiding officer refers to himself as *the Chair.* Other terms which are used to describe the Chair, such as *Chairperson* are legal only when the bylaws so specify, and then are considered substandard.

Debatable • May be discussed. Some motions are not debatable.

Committee • One or more persons, appointed or elected, to investigate, report, or take action on particular subjects and questions. There are standing committees and special committees.

Constitution • A document containing the rules that the organization has adopted for the management of its affairs.

Consideration • Discussion, debate, vote.

Consideration by committee • Discussion, debate, examination of referred matter.

Debate • Discussion following the Chair's stating a debatable motion.

Decision • A ruling by the Chair or by the assembly. The parliamentarian advises the Chair, the Chair rules.

Decorum • Appropriateness of conduct in meetings. Courtesy and decency towards other members during debate and conduct of business.

Division of the assembly • Call for a rising vote to visually verify a voice vote. This is not a motion for a count of the votes. If a count is desired, a motion to count the vote must be adopted.

Division of the question • A motion consisting of more than one part, each part capable of standing alone, may be divided; that is, debated and voted on separately.

En gros • (In gross) Consideration as a whole. Opposite of seriatim.

Ex officio • By virtue of the office. The president is not a member ex officio of any committee unless such privilege has been granted in special rules or by the bylaws. Temporary officers do not assume ex officio duties.

Fix • In parliamentary terminology: to place definitely.

Floor, Obtaining the • A member is recognized by the Chair and granted the privilege of speaking.

General consent • May be called for by the Chair when there does not appear to be opposition to the question, or when there is no objection. Also called unanimous consent.

General orders • Questions postponed to a certain day or meeting. Bylaw amendments are General Orders as well.

Germane • Closely related, pertinent. All remarks must be germane to the subject being discussed. A primary amendment must be germane to the pending motion and a secondary amendment must be germane to the primary amendment.

Honorary • The title Honorary Member or Honorary Officer may be conferred upon a person only when the bylaws permit such a title.

Immediately pending question • The most recent motion introduced upon which no action has been taken.

Lost motion • A motion rejected by vote. A tie vote defeats a motion when a majority vote is required.

Main motion • A motion which brings a matter before the assembly for consideration and action.

Meeting • An assembly of members of a deliberative body to transact business or participate in a program.

Minutes • The official record of business transacted by an organization at each regular, special or annual meeting, or convention of delegates.

Motion • A proposal or proposition that the assembly take certain action or express itself as holding certain opinions.

Null and void • Having no legal effect. Invalid.

Order of business • The list of official business to come before the assembly, beginning with approval of the minutes and ending at the finish of new business.

Orders of the day • Usually the regular order of business, when classes of subjects are taken up in a particular order.

Out of order • Not in order. In violation of the rules of the organization or of the parliamentary authority adopted by the members.

Pending • Undecided or unresolved.

Pending question • A motion which has been stated by the Chair, and upon which no action has been taken.

Preamble • Introduction to a resolution. A preamble may be a brief statement of background.

Precedence • Established order of priority of motions. Rank.

Prevailing side • The side receiving the greatest number of votes. May be the affirmative side or the negative side.

Previous notice • As the bylaws or adopted rules of order specify. May be given at the previous meeting, by mail to all members, or in the call to meeting.

Pro tem • Pro tempore. Temporarily. For the time being. A member serving in the absence of the regular officer, chairman, or secretary is said to be serving pro tem.

Proxy • A power of attorney or written authorization for one member to act for another.

Putting the question • Taking the vote.

Question • The question is on adopting or rejecting the immediately pending motion.

Quorum •The *Quorum* is the minimum number of members who must be present in order that business may be legally transacted. If the bylaws do not specify otherwise, a quorum is a majority of the members.

Receive • Receive a report. The *hearing* of a report presented either in writing or orally. No action is required unless recommendations are included and moved. The reporting member moves the adoption of the *recommended* action. No motion is required to hear a report.

Resolution • A formal motion, which may include a preamble. A resolution should be in writing. Use the term *Resolved* instead of *I move*.

Rules of order • Written parliamentary rules adopted by the members. Usually the parliamentary authority is a manual such as *Robert's Rules of Order Newly Revised.*

Second • Indicates that a second member is willing to consider a motion.

Secondary motions • Subsidiary, privileged, and incidental motions.

Seriatim • One after another in a series. To consider seriatim is to consider section by section or paragraph by paragraph. After all sections have been considered, one vote is taken on the entire document.

Session • A meeting, or series of connected meetings such as a convention.

Sine die • Without day. Used at the end of convention.

Speaker • The person who has been assigned the floor.

Special meeting • A meeting called between regular meetings for a special purpose. Notice must be given to all members of the time, place, and purpose of the special meeting. Only business specified in the notice may be transacted.

Special orders • A motion or subject assigned to a certain time, and made a special order by a two-thirds vote.

Special rules of order • Rules, adopted by a two-thirds vote after notice, that modify the parliamentary authority.

Standing rules • Administrative rules that are usually of a semi-permanent or temporary nature.

Statutes • Laws enacted by state and local governments.

Sustain • Uphold the ruling of the Chair.

Tellers • Persons appointed or elected to count the votes and to report to the assembly.

The special order for the meeting • A question for which an entire meeting is reserved. Questions to be taken up at a Special meeting for which notice have been given are The Special Orders for the meeting.

Vive voce • A voice vote.

Vote • The expression of the will of the assembly.

> *Majority vote* - more than half the votes cast.
>
> *Plurality* - the largest number of votes cast.
>
> *Two-thirds* - at least two thirds of the votes cast.
>
> *Tie vote* - the same number of negative and affirmative votes.
>
> *Unanimous consent* - no objection
>
> > (also called General Consent)
>
> *Unanimous vote* - no dissenting votes. This does not mean that everyone voted on the question, but that those on the opposing side did not vote at all.

Yield • Accede to, relinquish. Motions yield to other motions of higher rank. A member may not yield any unexpired portion of his time in debate to another member. The right to the floor for debate is not transferable.

Test yourself, page 96, #16

FOR ADDITIONAL STUDY
Look for the answers in this workbook and in Robert's Rules of Order Newly Revised.

1. Define the principles and purposes of parliamentary law and procedure.
2. What are the four principal types of deliberative assemblies?
3. What characteristics of committees are not characteristics of an assembly?
4. Why does an organization need rules?
5. Name four types of rules that a society may formally adopt.
6. Give eight standard characteristics of the Main Motion.
7. Write a resolution with two preamble paragraphs and two resolving paragraphs.
8. How many amendments to the main motion may be pending at one time?
9. If the motion "Previous Question" is pending, may the Main Motion be laid on the table?
10. Why are privileged motions privileged?
11. Which motions are amendable but are not debatable?
12. Define quorum.
13. What action can be taken in the absence of a quorum?
14. When may the chair vote?
15. What is the difference between "order of business" and "an order of the day"?
16. Define "general orders" and "special orders."
17. What is the method of counting a rising vote?
18. Describe a roll call vote.
19. When may the vote be interrupted?
20. Give two methods of absentee voting.
21. Name five methods of nomination.
22. When does an election take effect?
23. What is the minimum number of officers?
24. When the president and vice-presidents are absent, who calls the meeting to order?
25. Describe "special committee."
26. What may a committee report contain?
27. What may a member do if the chair ignores a point of order?
28. Why is it not wise to adopt an entire committee report?
29. What is the result of a tie vote?
30. How does one address the chair to gain recognition?
31. How does the chair announce the result of the vote?
32. Define "recess."
33. Which motions require a two-thirds vote for adoption?
34. Which of the thirteen ranking motions are undebatable?
35. Define "a second" to the motion.

Questions for additional study
Intermediate level
Look for the answers in *Roberts Rules of Order Newly Revised*

1. In a meeting where a quorum is present, who may call attention to the fact that members have left and the quorum has been lost?

2. May an order of business be in any sequence that the society desires?

3. Are advance copies of the minutes of a meeting mailed to members before the next regular meeting the official minutes?

4. When do minutes become the official minutes of a meeting?

5. If an officer reporting a recommendation regarding his office should not move the implementation of the recommendation, may another officer do so?

6. May an officer make the motion to implement the recommendations of a committee of which he is chairman?

7. When a time limit has been established on speeches in debate, does the time limit apply to the reporting member of a committee while giving his report?

   Does the time limit apply to the reporting member of a committee in discussing the merits of the committee recommendation?

8. When an election is held by voice vote and nominations are from the floor, are all candidates voted on?

9. When there are two candidates for one office to be filled, is it a legal ballot when the voter votes yes for one and no for the other?

10. When there are two candidates for one office to be filled, and a member marks the ballot with a *no* for one of the candidates, is that considered a *yes* vote for the other one?

11. Is an election to fill a vacancy in an office a general order or a special order?

12. When the president is absent, who presides, the vice-president or the president-elect? Explain the circumstances under which either would preside.

13. When notice has been given of a bylaw amendment, does the proposed amendment become a general order or a special order?

14. The bylaws of an organization prescribe that there shall be a president, a first vice-president, a second-vice-president, a third-vice-president, a secretary, and a treasurer. A bylaws amendment proposes to strike out "a first vice-president and a second vice-president, and the word 'third'." What occurs when an amendment to the proposed bylaw amendment is adopted to strike out "a first vice-president"?

Bibliography

Demeter, George. *Demeter's Manual of Parliamentary Law and Procedure*. Boston: Little, Brown, 1969.

Robert, Sarah Corbin, et al. *Robert's Rules of Order Newly Revised*. Glenview, Ill.: Scott, Foresman, 1990.

Suggested Additional Reading

Robert, Henry M. *Parliamentary Law*. New York: Irvington. Bicentennial Ed., 1975.

Robert, Henry M. *Parliamentary Practice*. New York: Irvington. Bicentennial Ed., 1975.

Stephens, Joyce L. *Guide For the Presiding Officer*. Clearwater, Florida: Frederick, 1990.

Stephens, Joyce L. *Guide to Voting*. Clearwater, Florida: Frederick, 1993.

Order form

Basic Parliamentary Procedure Workbook, 5th Ed. 1994	____@ $15.95 ea.	_____
Guide For The Presiding Officer	____@ $19.95 ea.	_____
Guide to Voting Procedures	____@ $24.95 ea	_____

Any 2 or more books, deduct 10% discount

Florida Residents please add applicable sales tax   _____

                                      Total   _____

Postage, shipping, handling
One book $3.00
    Additional books add $.50 each postage and handling   _____

                                 Total enclosed   _____

Name _____

Address _____

State _____Zip Code_____Phone_____

Organization _____

    Mail to:
    Frederick Publishers
    P. O. Box 5043
    Clearwater, FL 34618
    Information (813) 530-3978

Guide For The Presiding Officer
ISBN 0-9629765-0-4
Answers to those 'getting started' questions
Tips for handling your new position
Tips and language for handling the order of business
Writing and using a script agenda
Language of the presider for all situations
Examples, Glossary of terms, Common errors to avoid
How to handle motions and resolutions
Motions charts
Motions that are out of order
Types of meetings, Voting
How to handle an election
Duties of officers, directors, and committees
Biblio
Index

Guide to Voting Procedures
for Voluntary Organizations
ISBN 0-9629765-3-9
A single source for information on voting procedures
All forms of voting explained
Numerous examples and illustrations
Biblio
Index